In *Moments 'til Midnight*, Brent draws some practical and power-ful lessons for students today from the life of the apostle Paul, who is by any measure one of the most influential people of all time. This book has a wonderful balance of stories, theol-ogy, and practical wisdom. As soon as it is out, I want a copy for my own teenage son.

Sean McDowell, author, apologist, and assistant professor of Apologetics, Biola University

Brent's book *Moments 'til Midnight* provides a fresh perspective on one of the most fascinating leaders ever to live, the apostle Paul. The book is a powerful reminder that all of us, just like Paul, are simply trying to live and lead well. *Moments 'til Midnight* helps our "want to" become our "how to," so that we can live each day with purpose and with a sacred sense of intentionality to redeem every moment on the journey.

Brad Lomenick, founder of BLINC and author of H3 *Leadership* and *The Catalyst Leader*

Considering what the last hours of the apostle Paul's life might have been like, *Moments 'til Midnight* takes us through his life, theology, and passions. Biblically faithful and practically helpful, I read the book in a single day, anticipating the next chapter. Brent Crowe has a gift for writing, and it is on full display in this gem.

Daniel L. Akin, president, Southeastern Baptist Theological Seminary

The pages of this book are filled with fresh and relevant truths that I will carry with me for years to come. It will encourage you to let your own life mirror Paul's unwilling-ness to relent in sharing the gospel, no matter the situation. *Moments 'til Midnight* is thought-provoking, filled with wisdom, and gives us the timely message that as believers in Jesus, this world is not our home.

Bethany Barr Phillips, worship leader

Brent Crowe writes from a unique perspective. His use of visual imagery and strong theology resonate in my heart as I empathize with Paul in his last few hours. With themes like grace, redemption, transformation, and forgiveness, I found myself, my story throughout its pages. And where I didn't find myself and wish I would have, it inspired me to press on and endure. You will find your story somewhere in the pages of this book, and Brent's writing will inspire you and encourage you in taking the next step on your journey with Jesus.

Matt Roberson, lead pastor,
The MET Church in Houston, Texas

Moments 'til Midnight is more than a captivating title; it is a calling to have a captivating testimony. Dr. Brent Crowe has done it once more with yet another resource that inspires us all on our Jesus journey to make our life count, not just through daily moments, but divine moments. Counting the cost begins with knowing we are not promised tomorrow; therefore, don't do tomorrow what God has told you to do today.

Ed Newton, pastor
Community Bible Church, San Antonio, Texas

I'm a huge fan of the apostle Paul and, now, a huge fan of Brent Crowe's writing. In Moments 'til Midnight, Crowe paints a picture of Paul's life and final hours that deeply impacted me—and I'm convinced it will impact you too. Packed with biblical insights and practical takeaways, this book is a must-read for anyone who wants to, like the great apostle, live a life for the maximum glory of God and the exponential advancement of his kingdom. Sir Francis Bacon once said, "Some books are to be tasted, others to be swallowed, and some few to be chewed and digested." Devour, digest, and enjoy this wonderfully powerful book.

Greg Stier, founder and CEO of
Dare 2 Share (dare2share.org)

MOMENTS 'til MIDNIGHT

BRENT CROWE

MOMENTS 'til MIDNIGHT

The Final Thoughts of a Wandering Pilgrim

PUBLISHING GROUP

NASHVILLE, TENNESSEE

To the amazing men affectionately known as B.O.B.

Thanks for helping me journey well. May we continue to encourage and serve one another until that day when we reach the heaven country.

Contents

Introduction

Paul the Pilgrim

The apostle Paul was, without a doubt, one of history's giants. Billions of people two millennia later still feel his impact. And while we could elaborate on and on about the roles he filled through his many adventures, maybe a holistic survey of the life he lived allows us to view him through a different paradigm. Could it be that the apostle Paul was a pilgrim on a simple and sacred quest? Yes, this quest would be an unlikely journey full of all the drama and violence necessary to keep any reader's attention. But you see, in the end, he was simply a pilgrim wandering on his way home the best he could.

I believe the more we interact with Paul, the clearer the picture becomes of a pilgrim consumed with his pilgrimage. An undeniable thread of all-encompassing purpose demonstrating the progress of a pilgrim is woven throughout his life, beginning even before the Damascus road conversion and evident with each step along the missionary journeys and each word penned as holy writ. It is clear from his own pen that Paul journeyed through "the wilderness of this world" with his eyes wide open;[1] all while making his way to a heavenly home:

- "For me, to live is Christ and to die is gain. Now if I live on in the flesh, this

1

means fruitful work for me; and I don't know which one I should choose. I am torn between the two. I long to depart and be with Christ—which is far better—but to remain in the flesh is more necessary for your sake. Since I am persuaded of this, I know that I will remain and continue with all of you for your progress and joy in the faith, so that, because of my coming to you again, your boasting in Christ Jesus may abound" (Phil. 1:21–26).

- "But our citizenship is in heaven, and we eagerly wait for a Savior from there, the Lord Jesus Christ" (Phil. 3:20).

- "So if you have been raised with Christ, seek the things above, where Christ is, seated at the right hand of God. Set your minds on things above, not on earthly things. For you died, and your life is hidden with Christ in God. When Christ, who is your life, appears, then you also will appear with him in glory" (Col. 3:1–4).

This pilgrim's journey is on full Technicolor display for all to see, but what impact does this have on modern-day followers of Jesus? Many of us would clearly say we follow Jesus but in the next breath would admit this "pilgrim" thing is a bit of a foreign or odd concept. Before that question can be answered—which is the endeavor of this book—let's first grasp a firmer understanding of what it means to be a modern-day pilgrim.

Rediscovering a Pilgrim's Identity

Blessed is the man whose
strength is in You, whose heart is
set on pilgrimage. (Ps. 84:5 NKJV)

I believe there is a pilgrim in each of us that is just longing to go on a journey. Arguably, the greatest challenge facing
us is to discover this identity, embrace it, and unleash it with
glorious celebration.

Helen Keller once said, "Life is a daring adventure . . . or
nothing at all."

We are part of that ancient tradition of people who
believed that Jesus of Nazareth was infinitely more than a
renegade rabbi from the backside of nowhere. And we believe
in the depths of our souls that following Jesus is the daring
adventure that makes up the pilgrimage of our lives. For we
are pilgrims wandering on our way home.

You were created for such an endeavor, and to deprive life
of this sense of pilgrimage is to miss out on so much of life's
purpose. I would go so far as to say that if you were to pause
in the chaos of your present life, take a deep breath, and read
the Bible a bit, you would discover: *a pilgrim you are, and a pilgrim
you were meant to be*. In this book we are going to let one of the
most respected pilgrims, and the thoughts he wrote down,
speak life into our own journeys. But, before we dive in, let's
elaborate a bit more on this word.

The dictionary defines *pilgrim* as "a person who journeys,
especially a long distance, to some sacred place as an act of
religious devotion; a traveler or wanderer, especially in a
foreign place."[2] While the definition is adequate, it is lacking
for those who are on a journey, a pilgrimage, of following
Jesus. Possibly my favorite Scripture that describes who we
are as pilgrims comes from Hebrews 11:13–16. Before seeing

those verses, we should know that the writer of Hebrews has spent the better part of the chapter describing and outlining Old Testament pilgrims who lived by faith and therefore were able to accomplish amazing things for God. The following verses are a description of those who believe in and greatly trust God with their lives.

> Each one of these people of faith died not yet having in hand what was promised, but still believing. How did they do it? They saw it way off in the distance, waved their greeting, and accepted the fact that they were *transients in this world*. People who live this way make it plain that they are looking for their true home. If they were homesick for the old country, they could have gone back any time they wanted. But they were after a far better country than that—*heaven* country. You can see why God is so proud of them, and has a City waiting for them. (Heb. 11:13–16 MSG, emphasis added)

The King James Version, in verse 13, called these people of faith "strangers and pilgrims on earth." So much can be gained from this one text when defining a pilgrim, but hopefully one truth is overwhelmingly clear: *people who place their faith in Jesus are pilgrims journeying through this world toward their heavenly home.*

Let's break this definition down into four bite-sized pieces.

1. *A pilgrim is consumed with the understanding that his/her life is all about a journey or pilgrimage.* If *pilgrim* is our identity, then it is safe to

say we were created for this journey. We are "transients in the world" or rather "temporary residents" on Earth. It is a sobering thought to ponder that everything about my life takes place within the context of this identity. In short, nothing in my life can or should be divorced from my view of Jesus, who has given me this identity. If pilgrim is who I am, then how I journey determines how I live.

2. *A pilgrim is willing to exhaust his/her resources to journey well.* If we have established that our identity is that of a pilgrim and all of life happens within the context of a pilgrimage, then it makes sense to steward our resources with the journey and the destination in mind. Jesus taught, "But store up for yourselves treasures in heaven, where neither moth nor rust destroys, and where thieves don't break in and steal. For where your treasure is, there your heart will be also" (Matt. 6:20–21). While Jesus is not teaching against earthly possessions, He is teaching how to have a heavenly perspective. The manner in which we use our earthly resources should be consistent with the priorities of heaven. If our hearts long for the things/possessions of this world, then we will get continually bogged down in the journey; but if our temporary possessions are viewed as instruments to move us onward toward our permanent

place, then our ultimate treasure will be Jesus and all that heaven has to offer. In short, what truly matters to the pilgrim are not things that can be consumed by moths, corroded by rust, or confiscated by thieves.

3. *A pilgrim believes that one journey can change the world.* All those mentioned in a positive manner in Hebrews 11 impacted their world for the glory of God. Abel presented a righteous gift to God. Enoch pleased God so much that God allowed him to bypass death and go straight to heaven. Noah obeyed God and built an ark. Abraham, by faith, obeyed God and received a son. Sarah, despite being infertile, gave birth to a son and a nation. Isaac, Jacob, and Joseph demonstrated faith in God's promises toward Israel. Moses led the nation of Israel. Rahab, a pagan prostitute, feared God and protected the Hebrew spies, thus aiding in Israel's defeat of Jericho—not to mention becoming part of Christ's lineage! Many more could be named, but the picture is clear: each one was identified as a pilgrim, and all of them changed their world.

4. *A pilgrim lives with the tension between the present journey and the destination.* Pilgrims live on the rugged road of the redeemed with the knowledge and anticipation of the glorified state that is restoration. In other

words, we know there is a real day on God's calendar in which He will make all things new again. A real day when God "will wipe away every tear from their eyes. Death will be no more; grief, crying, and pain will be no more" (Rev. 21:4). In the meantime we live and journey through a world where pain, tears, and death are a reality. We live as those redeemed but not yet restored. Each pilgrim, then, should look forward toward heaven to inform the manner in which we live on Earth.

And so we must journey through the wilderness of this world as temporary sojourners. For some, the heavenly country is just around the bend; for others, the road is much longer. For all of us, heaven is a home that is both close and far. A home with God's desired will on full display. A home we were meant for all along.

Let Us Imagine

What we are about to discuss is simply a creative exercise of the mind, an effort to study the life and journey of Paul in a fresh way. For the next part to work, you as the reader must be willing to tap into that God-given gift called imagination.

Deep breath . . .

Imagination engaged . . .

Here we go.

Noon

Come, Let Us Wonder Together

Set the Stage

It wasn't his first trip to Rome, but it would be his last. Paul had become such a threat and a nuisance that the brutal dictator Nero could no longer tolerate the presence of his kind in the empire. Thus, in the most powerful city in the world, one of history's giants would be thrown into jail for the last time.

Nero was too late though, for the life that preceded one last court hearing and one last incarceration had already put into motion all that was necessary to alter the course of history. The message that burned in Paul would not be stopped because the mission of God could not fail. Emperor Nero, who had earned his cruel reputation, was no match for the Creator of all, who makes empires rise and fall without even exerting Himself.

Nero was one bad dude whose ledger was littered with blood as a result of one sadistic decision after another. It is believed that his mother had his stepfather Claudius I murdered so that her teenage son could be crowned emperor.

Some years later Nero would in turn have his mother murdered, as well as his wife, so he could marry a woman with
whom he was having an affair, whom he would also later
have murdered. It was readily understood that to cross Nero
in any way was to take one's life into one's own hands. He
had the ability, for a short time, to snuff out any plots against
him with violent and ruthless revenge.

One of the more historic moments of his rule was the
great fire of Rome in AD 64, which destroyed much of the
city. The fire would last for more than a week, destroying
three, and damaging seven more, of the fourteen districts in
Rome. Many historians believe Nero orchestrated the fire so
that he could rebuild the city as he saw fit, including a gold
palace for himself. Nero, looking for a scapegoat, blamed the
fire on Christians and subsequently began a wave of violent
persecution against them.

Early Christian theologian and author Tertullian cred-
its Nero for ushering in an age of persecution that would
continue for approximately two hundred years. Followers of
Jesus would be persecuted across the Roman Empire until
AD 313 when Constantine decriminalized Christian worship.
Nero would commit suicide in AD 68 during a revolt against
his leadership. The martyrdom of the apostle Paul took place
sometime after the great fire and before Nero's death.

It's odd when you think about it: Nero began to think
of himself as divine in his mid-twenties, which must be the
pinnacle of arrogance for someone who has fallen in love
with his own fame. And yet, despite this, he felt threatened
by a humble people who spent their lives at the feet of Jesus
and were known for loving one another. Yes, Christians were
Nero's scapegoat for the great fire, but it wasn't just because
they were easy prey; rather it was because this movement led
by men like Paul and Peter could not be controlled. It stood

in direct contradiction to the cancerous paganism that had infiltrated and was destroying the souls of Nero's citizens.

Nero hated Christianity because the existence of this so-called "cult" stood in passive defiance of his leadership and authority. Nero thought himself to be a god, but the good news of this movement and its messengers seemed to say to him, "Yet for us there is one God, the Father. All things are from him, and we exist for him. And there is one Lord, Jesus Christ. All things are through him, and we exist through him" (1 Cor. 8:6).

While Paul could be bound with chains, the message to which he had dedicated his life continued to spread unencumbered. The ten thousand miles this feeble man, now in his sixties, had traveled by land and sea over the previous thirty years could not be erased. He knew all too well what Nero did not, for Paul himself had begun his career—not unlike Nero—by trying to stamp out the fire of Christianity.

He, however, discovered what we in this present day can easily observe: to persecute followers of Jesus only furthers the movement. So, on the road to Damascus, Paul (also called Saul) came face-to-face with the renegade rabbi known as Jesus of Nazareth. It not only brought him to his knees, it brought him to saving faith. In that moment—a moment that would determine all of his future moments—Paul made two discoveries: "Jesus Christ was alive and Saul of Tarsus was dead in sin and a total failure in himself."[1] On a dusty road, in an effort to halt the ever-growing sect of Christ followers, a well-educated Pharisee with a prestigious heritage from a well-to-do family became a follower of the person he thought to be cursed and dead. In that moment everything changed.

Following his conversion, Paul dedicated his life to advancing the movement of Christianity. He would lead three

extensive missionary journeys that would take him throughout much of the first-century world. He was an apostle who
would plant churches, train pastors, and write thirteen letters
under the inspiration of the Holy Spirit that are preserved in
the New Testament. He was a masterful theologian, strategist,
communicator, and preacher. He was a man driven by the
grace of Jesus, which had transformed his life. In fact, grace
would be referenced more than one hundred times in his
writings—more than any other concept—and always appear-
ing in the greeting and benediction of his letters.

Historian John Pollock wrote of Paul's motivation in his
work The Apostle: A Life of Paul: "Paul could not restrict himself
to one city. No man in previous history had traveled so far
or suffered so much to bring men truth; he could not stay
still or silent while others remained ignorant of the Word of
Truth, and the Life. Every day he told all about Jesus and His
resurrection."[2]

In our time Paul is known as the great leader, apostle
to the Gentiles, and the individual who is responsible for
the gigantic advancement of our faith. Theologians agree,
"By the time the New Testament period comes to an end,
Christianity is a worldwide, Gentile-dominated religion. Paul
is in no small measure responsible for that transformation."[3]
But during his day he was known as a fugitive, a man who
ultimately had been brought up on charges for propagating
an illegal religion in a culture that esteemed emperor worship. And, of course, this was a capital crime. And so it is
that, for the purposes of this book, we meet up with Paul at
the end of his life, wasting away in a Roman dungeon called
the Mamertine Prison.

Paul was no stranger to suffering, having endured long
hardships and:

far worse beatings, many times near death.
Five times I received forty lashes minus one
from Jews. Three times I was beaten with
rods. Once I received a stoning. Three times
I was shipwrecked. I have spent a night and
a day in the open sea. On frequent journeys,
I faced dangers from rivers, dangers from
robbers, dangers from my own people, dangers from the Gentiles, dangers in the city,
dangers in the wilderness, dangers at sea,
and dangers among false brothers; toil and
hardship, many sleepless nights, hunger and
thirst, often without food, cold, and without
clothing. (2 Cor. 11:23–27)

And certainly Paul was no stranger to imprisonment,
having probably spent five to six years of his ministry and
adult life incarcerated. Yet every brush with death, beating,
and prison stay somehow seemed mild compared to the cold
dark stone of this Roman dungeon.

Here Paul wrote and finished his final instructions—the
last letter he would ever write—to a young man he loved
like a son. Knowing these were his final words, it was a tear-
filled and sobering task that probably caused him more than
once to pause and collect himself. And once the letter was
completed, one gets the sense from reading 2 Timothy, Paul
knew his death was near.

As the streets of Rome bustled with a whirlwind of activity, the apostle Paul sat beneath, chained in a dungeon. While
the exact details surrounding the execution and timing of his
death are unknown and lost in the annals of history, in the
manner of his execution we can have more confidence. He
was in all likelihood taken and beheaded outside of Rome in

a common place for execution along the Ostian Road in June of AD 67.

What if sometime after the completion of his second letter to Timothy, Paul learned one late morning that his execution would be carried out at midnight? Paul had the miraculous habit of turning the most unlikely of enemies into friends and co-laborers in the faith. Therefore, would it be that much of a stretch to think that he had endeared himself to one of the Roman guards assigned to watch over him? One could even imagine that this guard had heard of the apostle who enjoyed Roman citizenship and was once a Pharisee employed by the Sanhedrin. And if one ponders long enough, it is certainly imaginable that a Roman soldier assigned to Paul might have converted to Christianity. He could have gone about his daily routine keeping watch over the dungeon, and at night gathered with other believers for church in the vast underground network referred to as the catacombs. There, in the subterranean passageways beneath the city, he may have borne witness of Paul to fellow believers.

The dungeon was growing warmer and seemingly soggier by the day, making the stench unbearable. Late spring was settling in and offering faint previews of the coming attraction that would be a hot summer. In the minutes close to the noon hour, a whisper comes down through the opening in the ceiling, which was the only way in or out of the dungeon prototype of hell. The whisper of the converted Roman solider was so faint at first that neither Paul nor the other inmates noticed. Then, in a more desperate effort to be heard, the man's voice became louder and more coarse. You know the kind of whisper that rises to the volume of a normal conversation—in an attempt to keep the whisper going, the speaker mutters out words that sound like sandpaper being muffled. This got Paul's attention and he looked up.

The soldier was lowering a bucket, and his words seemed to imply that it contained an important message. In an effort to conceal this illegal activity, the guard had smuggled a message into the bucket of food that was for the prisoners that day. When the bucket reached the dungeon floor, sure enough, right on top of the slop, was a torn piece of parchment folded in half. Paul delicately picked up the note, retreated to a wall where he had been propping himself up that morning, and opened the correspondence. It simply read: EXECUTION TO BE CARRIED OUT AT MIDNIGHT. Signed: *Your brother on the journey.*

Sitting alone in that dark and damp place where it seemed that every stone had been infected by blood or some other bodily fluid, Paul now knew the exact time his pilgrimage would come to an end. The walls of the dungeon seemed to cry out with a history of pain and hopelessness. And yet, even though the immediate environment was less than ideal, the next step of the journey had been a lighthouse of hope guiding Paul homeward for years. He may have been in a dungeon, but he was soon to be raised up and seated in the heavenly places with Jesus.

Just feet beneath the streets of the most powerful city in the world, Paul now sits alone with his thoughts. He had no more letters to write, no more churches to plant, no more sermons to preach, and no more missionary journeys to go on. He will never watch another sunrise, only observe the distant sunset. He will never again feel the comforting embrace of a co-laborer or lose time around a warm fire talking the evening away. He will never feel the sea breeze on his face pulling out of a harbor to pioneer new territory for the gospel. No, on this last day, the best Paul could hope for was the Roman guards to allow Luke, his friend and doctor, to visit him—if only for a few minutes.

What did this pilgrim wandering his way home think about in those final hours before his execution? It's amazing how much the brain can remember or recall in a short amount of time. I guess our minds are more like picture galleries than data banks with spreadsheets of information. Paul's first thoughts would have been drawn to the theme he wrote most about—grace—and how his life was transformed from one of potential to one of purpose. He tells Timothy in their final correspondence: "Remember Jesus Christ, risen from the dead and descended from David, according to my gospel" (2 Tim. 2:8).

Throughout each passing hour, Paul's mind's eye could have focused on a variety of other factors: friends and community, loneliness, a heavenly mind-set, godly living, unity of the church, his belief that with God all things are possible, the countless people he influenced through the art of letter writing, how grace demands more and how God works in our failures, his journey as a story well told and a life worth imitating.

While books upon books could be filled with potential thoughts and in-depth analysis of Paul's life, these topics have been chosen for the purposes of modern-day pilgrims. In the following pages we are going to allow one pilgrim's journey to echo through the ages into a lot of other pilgrim's journeys. So that we can wander well, as temporary sojourners, because we inherited the wisdom of a pilgrim that finished well. So come and

> Let us wonder together.
>
> Let us learn and discover.
>
> Let us ask questions and wrestle with answers.
>
> Let us resolve to live with a profound sense of purpose . . .

so that we may journey through this world with our
    eyes wide open
and make our way home, to THE home,
the place where all pilgrims arrive after a lifetime of
    wandering.

One O'clock
Only the Sinner

"Christ Jesus came into the world to save sinners"—and I am the worst of them. (1 Tim. 1:15)

Every story has a dominant theme, an undeniable idea that rises to the surface above all others. The best of stories have redemption as the centralized idea, made possible by a hero or team of heroes—a redeemer of sorts. Paul's was that kind of story.

His story had redemption as its theme and the Redeemer as the central character. And when one lives this kind of story, when one embarks on this kind of pilgrimage, one word stands out among them all: *grace*.

I have this friend who is an Anglican priest by day and a songwriter and performer by night. I first met Josh in college and have been listening to his music for the better part of fifteen years. I've always felt he is one of those artists that, at some point, we'll all be listening to. One of my favorite songs he has written is entitled "Only the Sinner." Here are some of the lyrics:

Only the sinner, only the weak
Only the man who lies and steals and cheats
Only the woman who runs around
Only the child with a selfish mouth
Only prostitutes and murderers
And crooked businessmen
Only those who have no alibi
Only those who cannot hide their sin

Only the dirty
Never the clean
Only the beggar men
Never the king
Only the messed up
Never the made, the made
Only the sinner
Jesus saves (written by Josh Bales)

I think Paul would have liked the lyrics to my friend's song. I think he would have found its message familiar and comforting. At one point in Jesus' ministry, the religious leaders criticized him for eating and keeping company with sinners. Our Savior's reply was at the heart of Paul's journey: "It is not those who are well who need a doctor, but those who are sick. I didn't come to call the righteous, but sinners" (Mark 2:17). Jesus came to be a friend to the sinner, *only those who have no alibi, only those who cannot hide their sin . . . only the messed up, never the made . . . only the sinner, Jesus saves.*

After his conversion in Acts 9, Paul lived a life full of purpose and mission. And while he was not held hostage by the guilt of his past sin, he never seemed to forget from what he had been forgiven. This is probably why Paul mentions grace more than any other word. Paul's soul had been made well, but he never forgot what it was like to be sin sick.

I like to read books—all kinds of books. Some of the more insightful things I've learned over the years have come from reading children's books to my kids or books like *All I Really Need to Know I Learned in Kindergarten* by Robert Fulghum. A friend gave me a copy in college, and I've read it from cover to cover a hundred times. It's basically a bunch of essays and quirky thoughts on life that use ordinary events to make you think about important ideas. During one such essay Fulghum writes about the age-old neighborhood game of hide-and-seek that is happening just outside his window. Observing the game, he writes,

> Did you have a kid in your neighborhood who always hid so good, nobody could find him? We did. After a while we would give up on him and go off, leaving him to rot wherever he was. Sooner or later he would show up, all mad because we didn't keep looking for him. And we would get mad back because he wasn't playing the game the way it was supposed to be played. There's *hiding* and there's *finding*, we'd say. And he'd say it was hide-and-seek, not hide-and-give-UP, and we'd yell about who made the rules and who cared about who, anyway, and how we wouldn't play with him anymore if he didn't get it straight and who needed him anyhow, and things like that. Hide-and-seek-and-yell. No matter what, though, the next time he would hide too good again. He's probably still hidden somewhere, for all I know.[1]

In many ways Paul was the kid that hid too well. He hid behind a graceless religion. The followers of Jesus feared him, making a point never to cross his path. The picture we have of Saul at the beginning of Acts 9 was a person who "was still breathing threats and murder against the disciples of the Lord." It is a picture of a man with growing success in stopping the movement of Jesus' followers. One scholar described him to be "like a warhorse who sniffed the smell of battle. He breathed on the remaining disciples the murder that he had already breathed in from the death of the others."[2] Saul was like a wild animal, a predator, and anyone who followed Jesus was his prey. In short he was a monster. This picture stands as a vivid reminder that *a life absent of grace will always lead to a tragic place.*

Saul was hiding, but he was hiding in plain sight. And while the example of Saul may seem more like the exception than the rule, I can assure you it is not. Many have tried to hide behind self-righteousness, which always arrives at the same inadequate conclusion. It's something we struggle with all too well in a Western, individualistic, do-it-yourself, "I can make it on my own," context. But there certainly isn't anything we can do to make ourselves more appealing or approved in God's eyes.

While I grew up in a great church environment, there was always a significant emphasis on *doing* and *doing more.* Memorize this many verses for a ribbon. Attend church this many times and you get recognized. Bring this many friends and you get a prize. The list goes on and on. There was always something to accomplish, and the more you accomplished, the more the spotlight was put on your accomplishments. I'm sure it was all driven by good intentions, but in a culture of earning credit, it almost felt like we were earning our Christianity. Of course, if I have to earn it, then God's grace is taken out of the equation. If my Christianity is based on *doing* and *doing more,* then self-righteousness takes center stage. And if self-righteousness takes the stage, it's no longer Christianity.

There is much to learn about grace from a guy who struggled with self-righteousness. So let's turn our attention to several big takeaways concerning grace in Paul's journey.

Jesus Is Grace Personified

Before his conversion, grace was a concept of which Saul was thoroughly ignorant. If grace was oxygen, Saul was suffocating. It would be analogous to an English-speaking person being dropped into a jungle tribe of people who only communicated by blinking their eyes at one another. One may know that people are communicating through eye blinks, but one is utterly confused. Saul was grace illiterate.

But after that fateful day on the road to Damascus, grace was transformed from being a foreign concept into a loving Savior. God's grace actually had a name, and it was Jesus. Now Saul was no longer persecutor; now he was an apostle— no longer ignorant but now illuminated, no longer a monster hunting down his prey but now a member of this movement, no longer hiding behind self-righteousness but now a sinner saved by grace.

> But God, who is rich in mercy, because of his great love that he had for us, made us alive with Christ even though we were dead in trespasses. You are saved by grace! He also raised us up with him and seated us with him in the heavens in Christ Jesus. (Eph. 2:4–6)

I guess grace could really be defined in the two little words at the beginning of this text: "But God." We were dead in our sins, *but God*. We were hiding behind self-righteousness, but God. But God is the grace of God interrupting our lives as if to say, "You deserve wrath, but I am 'mighty to save.'"

One of my favorite authors from yesteryear was J. C. Ryle, who was the first Anglican bishop of Liverpool in the late 1800s. He wrote a book titled *The True Christian*. In it he expounded on this idea of grace undeserved:

> He was not obliged to redeem us. . . . It is the grace of God that, when we were all without hope, Christ came into this world, to do things we never could have done, to fulfil that holy and just and good law which brings us all in guilty, and He did fulfil it to the last jot and tittle; to suffer the punishment we deserved, and He did suffer it up on the cross, and drank the bitter cup to the very dregs; and by the things He did and the things He suffered He provided a perfect righteousness for every one that is willing to believe.[3]

I say again, grace has a name, and it is Jesus, for Jesus is grace personified.

Grace Gives Peace

Paul began all his letters by praying grace and peace over his readers. For example, in Galatians 1:3 he writes: "Grace to you and peace from God the Father and our Lord Jesus Christ." One of the great fruits of a life experiencing God's grace is peace. The order in which Paul writes time and again is of significance in understanding the correlation—grace first and then peace. The grace of Jesus is always the prerequisite for experiencing the peace of God.

The grace of Jesus received in my life is the only way I can truly experience peace in a world filled with unrest. If Jesus is grace personified, then through the redemptive work of Christ, we were granted peace. One of the greatest examples of peace in the New Testament was how the gospel broke down the dividing wall between the Jews and the Gentiles. This text demonstrates peace from the inside out.

> For Christ himself has brought **peace** to us. He united Jews and Gentiles into one people when, in his own body on the cross, he broke down the wall of hostility that separated us. He did this by ending the system of law with its commandments and regulations. He made **peace** between Jews and Gentiles by creating in himself one new people from the two groups. (Eph. 2:14–15 NLT, emphasis added)

Because of grace, we can enjoy peace in our souls and peace with those around us. Grace gives peace inside and out.

We live in a world that seems to be tearing itself apart any way it can. For example, who would have thought that fifty years after the civil rights movement there would still be racial tension and prejudice in our country? When I was a kid, we studied about Dr. King in our history books, which seemed to imply that racial inequality was something of the past. The "I Have a Dream" speech is grainy black-and-white video footage, so doesn't that mean the issue is ancient history? It is entirely shameful that some individuals and systems still discriminate based on skin color but understandable when you know a little something about sin. Sin has a twisted and perverted way of reinventing itself. When we take our eyes off things that make for peace and operate on assumptions, sin gets a foothold. History books, museums, and grainy YouTube videos may have helped foster a mind-set that racism and prejudice in my country are old news. This might even lead one to assume we can put a check in the box next to that task. But my fear is that we've put a check mark in a box when the task was never completed.

So in this climate those of us who have been granted the grace of God should seek that which makes for peace. And by the way, we should never stop seeking that which makes for peace, for the moment we do we give opportunity for sinful assumptions to creep back in. Paul sums it up well in Romans 14:19, "So then, let us pursue what promotes peace and what builds up one another." In short, people who have received grace promote peace. If you are a Christian, and you enjoy peace in your soul and maybe even in your home, then become the person that helps your culture discover and enjoy peace as well.

We are people granted the grace of Jesus; therefore we are a people who get to enjoy, promote, and pursue peace. The pilgrim's journey will not be littered with memorials from battles won; rather, the road will be filled with stories of people who interacted with those who have grace and peace.

A friend of mine attended a concert years ago where Jimi Hendrix was the headliner. THE Jimi Hendrix—arguably the greatest electric guitar player in history! My friend, who wasn't a Christian at the time, was at the concert and on all kinds of drugs. Undeniably enjoying the event, the strangest thing happened in the middle of the set. Jimi stopped playing and just looked out into the crowd. He asked, "Anyone know where I can get some peace?"

My friend recalled that, in a room of four thousand people, most of whom were high on drink and drug, there was a stunned silence. A few moments later the concert resumed. Paul's life, or any pilgrim's journey for that matter, should answer that question. "Yeah Jimi, we got ourselves some peace, and we found it at the feet of Jesus."

Grace Gives Me Endurance

While many things about Paul's life are relatable to every modern-day pilgrim, some remarkable events will not and cannot be replicated. Somewhere near the top of the "remarkable events in Paul's life that the average person doesn't experience" list is the time he was privileged to go see heaven. Let me say that a different way. I'm not talking about when Paul died and went to heaven. Nope! There was a time about fourteen years before he wrote 2 Corinthians that he actually was given access to heaven.

One time I got to ride a roller coaster at a theme park before it was open to the public, and that was pretty amazing. But it was nothing compared to Paul's experience. And what he saw and heard in heaven was so astonishing and incredible that he couldn't even describe it in human language!

Now let me ask you a question: How do you go and see heaven, something no one else is allowed to do, and not think too highly of yourself? I mean, if I got a trip to heaven and then had another twenty years on Earth, I might be tempted to write a book about it or do a speaking tour where people would come and listen to me talk about seeing heaven. I would do interviews and answer questions. And all my responses would be laced with a perfected "humble brag." Why? Because I had been given an experience no one else was granted! Because I am more special than everyone else! And that's probably why I won't get a fast pass to heaven any time before I actually move there. And in all seriousness, God didn't want Paul to get the bighead either, which is why he wrote:

> Therefore, so that I would not exalt myself,
> a thorn in the flesh was given to me, a mes-
> senger of Satan to torment me so I would not
> exalt myself. Concerning this, I pleaded with
> the Lord three times that it would leave me.
> But he said to me, "My grace is sufficient for
> you, for my power is perfected in weakness."
> (2 Cor. 12:7–9)

Now no one knows exactly what Paul's "thorn in the flesh" means. Was it poor eyesight, malaria, epilepsy, or some other physical condition? Maybe it was more psychological in nature and could have been anxiety or depression. In any case Paul asked and pleaded with the Lord three times to take it away. Paul obviously felt the "thorn in the flesh" weakened him and thus hindered his ability to accomplish and endure the tasks associated with his calling. So, why did God give it to him? One scholar wrote: "The thorn punctured any pride that might surge within him because of his grand entry into heaven, and the result was that he dealt with others with the meekness and gentleness of Christ rather than with the arrogant puffery of Satan."[4]

God sometimes answers no to our requests so that in our journey we learn always to say a resounding YES! to His suffi- ciency. God's grace was enough for Paul to carry through any trial or persecution he would face. It did more than just make him humble; it made him endure because where Paul was weak, Jesus was sufficient. Grace is the fuel in our tank that will never run out. Paul demonstrates to us that God's grace not only saves us but sustains us. Grace is God's presence and thus His provision for every circumstance, no matter how difficult or how sharp the thorn may be.

In fact, saying yes to God's sufficiency positions us to know how God's *power is perfected in weakness.* I don't know about you, but I often feel inadequate and certainly insufficient before the Lord. How could God use such a sinner like me? I mean really, if you knew my past mistakes, you would put this book down right now! I may be the only one, but I have a sneaking suspicion that plenty of others feel the same way I do.

I think the Lord smiles a little when he hears such thoughts because in our weakness we become an excellent tool for the Lord.[5] Whether we are made weak by past sin or present physical conditions, God specializes in using the not-so-obvious candidate to show off His power.

The timing here is important. Paul spoke of his thorn in the flesh, how God's grace is sufficient and His "power is perfected in weakness" at the beginning of Paul's ministry. Though he was weak, God would enable him for the ten thousand miles of missionary journeys ahead. Though we are weak, God's grace is enough. God's grace gives us endurance so that we may journey onward, wandering daily in Christ's sufficiency.

Grace Makes Us Humble

So Paul had his "thorn in the flesh" to keep him humble that he might endure with the sufficiency of Jesus. So the question becomes, Did it work? Did the thorn in the flesh, giving him a better understanding of God's grace and sufficiency, keep him humble over the long haul? There is fascinating evidence to be found in his first letter to Timothy.

Keep in mind that when Paul wrote 1 Timothy, he had been living with his "thorn in the flesh" for over twenty years! In that letter he wrote, "This saying is trustworthy and deserving of full acceptance: 'Christ Jesus came into the world to save sinners'—and I am the worst of them" (1 Tim. 1:15). Paul is counting himself among the worst of the worst sinners. The Greek word translated "worst" is *prótos* and is usually translated "first," giving the notion that he is the most prominent or leading sinner.[6] Paul was saying, "I'm the first at being the worst!"

One of the things I appreciate so much from Paul's pilgrimage was that he stayed humble. As he neared the end of his life, he still realized his need for God's grace. I wonder if he thought about Jesus' dying on the cross for his sins and thought to himself, *I need the sacrificial love of God as much today as I did all those years ago on the Damascus road.* There is a lot to be learned here. Sometimes we act like the longer we follow Jesus, the less we need His grace. As if growing in our faith means we become more independent and self-reliant. Or maybe we fall prey to thinking we needed God's grace more when we were lost in our sins. We think back to all our wicked ways before we met Jesus and ponder, *Now that was a sinner who needed to be saved by grace!* This could be understood as a sort of spiritual arrogance. It's a dangerous place to be when we think we can pull Christianity off on our own. When we think we were saved by grace but will finish by works.

In reality the opposite is true. The longer we follow Jesus, the more we realize our need for grace. The more we think, *Now I am a sinner that still needs God's saving grace!* You see, maturity isn't about relying on God less; it's about relying more on what only God can offer our lives. The key to staying humble, it would seem, is knowing our insufficiency and living ever grateful for God's willingness to give us grace.

The great author and thinker C. S. Lewis wrote on the subject of humility in *Mere Christianity*, one of his most important books. In it he wrote that if you met a truly humble person, he or she would look different from any preconceived notions: "Probably all you will think about him is that he seemed a cheerful, intelligent chap who took a real interest in what you said to him. If you do dislike him, it will be because you feel a little envious of anyone who seems to enjoy life so easily. He will not be thinking about humility: he will not be thinking about himself at all."[7] I think Timothy could have seen a lot of Paul in Lewis's explanation of humility. And his humility is evidenced elsewhere when he calls himself "the least of all the saints" in Ephesians 3:8 and "the least of the apostles" in 1 Corinthians 15:9.

In short, God's grace makes us humble. Understanding grace leaves no other option than humility. And the more we know about the grace of Jesus, the less room we have in our lives for pride. Just as Paul grew in his faith, he also grew in his humility. The humblest people are not those who think of grace in the past tense: *I was a sinner saved by grace!* As if grace was only needed for a day. The humblest people are those who think of grace in the present tense: *I am a sinner saved and still needing God's saving grace.* Grace is not for a day; grace is something we need *every* day! So we grow in our humility not by concentrating on being humble but by realizing and walking in God's grace daily. Therefore, it could even be said that the humblest of individuals should be those who are closest on their pilgrimage to heaven country.

Grace Makes Us Quick to Forgive

Grace is forever amazing because grace is forever undeserved. And those who have experienced grace should be quick to extend it. To put it bluntly, *the forgiven FORGIVE!* We are a people who never forget what it was like to be given grace and thus be forgiven of our sin, so we are a people who in turn extend what was given to us.

Oswald Chambers said of forgiveness: "The thing that awakens the deepest well of gratitude in a human being is that God has forgiven sin. Paul never got away from this. When once you realize all that it cost God to forgive you, you will be held as in a vice, constrained by the love of God."[8] Three little words—I am forgiven—should create in us a well of gratitude that overflows to all those who intersect with our pilgrimage.

The Greek word that is translated forgive most of the time in the Paul's writing comes from the same root word as grace. Therefore, forgiveness is simply extending grace. A prime example of this is when Paul wrote in Colossians 3:13, "Just as the Lord has forgiven you, so you are also to forgive." It's easy for me to remember this Greek word for grace because it is the name we chose for my second daughter: Charis (cháris). And the word "to forgive" from the Greek charízomai means "to give or grant graciously and generously, with the implication of good will on the part of the giver—to give, to grant, to bestow generously."[9]

I don't mention the Greek in an effort to impress (truth be known I barely made it through my language classes in seminary). I include them to demonstrate that cháris is at the heart of charízomai—that is to say, biblically speaking, grace is at the heart of forgiveness.

The key to forgiving someone who has wronged you is not to try harder and harder and then eventually feel like you have forgiven them. NO! We don't work up forgiveness. If we can do it on our own, then grace isn't involved. The key to forgiving is found in your own forgiveness. The answer is not to pull yourself up by your bootstraps and try harder but to grow in an understanding of grace to the point where extending it only makes sense. I forgive, even my worst enemies, because the more I study grace, the more I realize that I was actually an enemy of God until He extended grace to me.

In some of Paul's final words, he was extending grace. In the end all but Luke had abandoned him. And at his final trial Paul writes in the closing lines of his last letter, "Everyone deserted me. May it not be counted against them" (2 Tim. 4:16). An absence of Christian friends did not lead Paul to harbor bitterness and disappointment, for those were burdens too heavy for this pilgrim to carry. He may have been poor by earthly standards, but he was rich in grace. Being so close to heaven, with his eyes fixed on glory, his pilgrimage was about to step foot into the land where each citizen had been forgiven. So with the land of forgiveness in clear sight, it would only make Christlike sense that forgiveness be granted to any and all who had wronged him.

Grace Teaches Me How to Love Well

In his book *The Grace of God*, Andy Stanley writes, "Grace acknowledges the full implication of sin and yet does not condemn."[10] We end our discussion on grace similar to where it began. That fact that we have been given grace is because of the finished work of Jesus. This is the love of God. So, if I have been given grace because God loves me, how then does grace teach me to love others?

First, God takes the initiative with grace; it is not something that can ever be earned or deserved. Stanley is again helpful when he writes, "To say that someone deserves grace is a contradiction in terms. You can no more deserve grace than you can plan your own surprise party. In the same way that planning voids the idea of surprise, so claiming to deserve voids the idea of grace. You can ask for it. You can plead for it. But the minute you think you deserve it, the "it" you think you deserve is no longer grace. It is something you have earned."[11] Just as God takes the initiative in surprising us with grace, so we should take the initiative in love. We do not love others because they deserve or earned it. Rather, we love simply because we have been loved. Grace teaches us to love by taking the initiative in loving others.

Grace also teaches us to love unconditionally. Living a life truly surprised by grace transforms the manner in which we love. Grace teaches me that I love others with no strings attached, with no agenda hiding in the shadows, and with no misguided expectations of what I could gain from loving. Grace teaches that I don't even love because it makes me feel good about myself; unconditional means I am not posturing to appear obedient.

Furthermore, grace teaches us to love completely. If Jesus is grace personified, then His sacrificial love on the cross demonstrates the extent to which God loves. God shows His graciousness toward us because through His Son "we have all received grace upon grace from his fullness . . . ; grace and truth came through Jesus Christ" (John 1:16–17). Christ so loved that He was completely obedient in His suffering, death, and triumphant resurrection. As one theologian put it, "Jesus Christ is God for us."[12] In Jesus, God is loving humanity, warts and all. In Jesus, God is loving not just the worst among us but also the worst in us. He knows we are sin sick through and through. We are the thief on the cross, the woman with the issue of blood, the demon-possessed man who hurts himself, and the half-dead man lying in a ditch on the side of the road between Jerusalem and Jericho. We are enemies, we are broken, we are sick, we are hopeless, and we are helpless. And in the midst of a pretty ugly scene, grace shows up. So much grace that it cannot be measured or even fully understood. So much grace that we are loved, the ugly parts and all. We are loved thoroughly; we are loved completely.

In the end there is always a part of the flesh that wants to claim credit for all that grace teaches us. We must fight this sense of pride and entitlement that points to trophies, first-place ribbons, or titles. The pilgrim making his way home doesn't have time to build memorials to what he has accomplished. Nor is there enough room in the luggage for our accolades. The pilgrim is simply awestruck that grace was given and grace was received. That idea was enough to consume a man like Paul for thirty-plus years; I think it can consume us all for a lifetime. And furthermore, can we just say for those in the cheap seats that hiding behind one's self-righteousness is exhausting. That feeling of never measuring up and always having to do more. I believe living with this weight of inadequacy, brought on by a chronic case of self-righteousness, was a burden God never intended humans to shoulder and is simply the result of sin and rebellion.

Oh, but when Paul got found, he got found indeed! As soon as he regained his sight and strength, "immediately he began proclaiming Jesus in the synagogues: 'He is the Son of God'" (Acts 9:20). He preached Jesus knowing that it was a death sentence for him. In fact, "After many days had passed, the Jews conspired to kill him" (Acts 9:23). Once he experienced grace, he went from the posture of a self-righteous terrorist killing in the name of religion to that of a pilgrim who found it impossible to compartmentalize the grace of God in his life. God's grace had infiltrated his being, and nothing in his life could separate him from it.

Two O'clock
From Potential to Purpose

Each day at schools all over the world, kids look forward to a moment in the schedule with eager anticipation. I am referring to none other than that glorious few minutes in the day called *recess*.

When I was a kid, recess was liberating for me. I didn't have to sit in a desk or concentrate or follow rules or look at math! No, for those few fateful moments, I was free! Free to run, free to play, free to talk at a volume above a whisper. I loved recess so much that when a grown-up would ask, "What's your favorite subject in school?" I would always reply with jubilee, "RECESS!"

I don't know if you remember recess at your school, but as soon as we stepped foot on the playground or rec fields, people would begin to navigate toward their respective activities. Some would go to the swings, others to the basketball courts, but most to a ragged old field where they would play an age-old game called kickball. Here they would commence to dividing up teams—which honestly, was as big a deal as playing the actual game. Thus, and unbeknown to a third-grade mind, choosing teams consumed a significant portion of recess. It was the daily event, and yet it was always predictable. The captains would choose the most popular or the most qualified kids first, leaving everyone else to feel like second-class citizens.

This process was a mixture of relief for some and humiliation for others as kids were chosen one by one. It also seemed that the whole process slowed with each passing pick for the crowd standing vulnerable before the captains. And as the crowd thinned, a sense of anxiety would begin to well up inside those not yet chosen. There would be an awkward silence, except for a little whispering among the already chosen ones. Meanwhile everyone else—the leftovers no one really wanted—were still waiting for their name to be called, asking themselves, *Am I going to be last?*

This humiliating exercise continued until there were only two kids left who had mustered up goofy grins on their faces in an effort to mask the pain and embarrassment they actually felt. One last name was called, and one last person was left unchosen. Then the captain would utter something like, "Well, I guess you're on our team." How humiliating! The final person wasn't even chosen, nor was his or her name called; that one was just leftover and by rule couldn't be left standing on the field as the game began.

On more than one occasion I've felt like the kid chosen last. And I think to some extent all of us have felt what it is like to be completely unwanted or unqualified. Most of us fall into the category that didn't include the popular kids. We tried to navigate those days with as much grace as we could muster, all the while knowing that the goofy grins on our faces actually masked a much deeper insecurity. Maybe that's why so many people liked The Hunger Games, a book trilogy that at one point even surpassed Harry Potter in sales. In some way we can relate to Katniss Everdeen living in

District 12. After all, anyone from the poorest district would certainly be the least likely candidate to lead a revolution.

> So to all the kids chosen last at recess
> To those who never seem to quite fit in at any chapter
>   in life
> For the folks who feel unqualified . . . or even unwanted
> To those who have more in common with Katniss than
>   the Capitol.

The pilgrimage of Paul, as he wandered on his way home to the heaven country, has something sacredly significant for your journey. You see Paul, even with all his potential, was the least likely candidate to lead a movement. Not a person alive thought, *You know the guy who has been assigned to imprison or kill everyone following Jesus? Yeah, that guy should be the one who leads the church in advancing the name of Jesus.* This is what is so amazing about Paul's journey. Jesus redeemed the guy with the worst résumé for the job. But once he was redeemed, his résumé was transformed.

Paul's life before the Damascus road—that is to say, all the preparation and potential, the graceless religion, and the violent reputation—only served to demonstrate that he was a trophy of grace set apart for God's purposes. In other words, God didn't waste Paul's past; he redeemed it so that Paul would live with purpose and on purpose.

The grace of God is that Jesus stands on the playgrounds of all of our lives and says, "I choose you first." And He doesn't choose us just so we can remain idle, as if being chosen was an end unto itself. No, we were chosen so now we live with purpose, as citizens of heaven navigating a broken world, as pilgrims making our way home. I wonder if sitting in that dungeon around the two o'clock hour, Paul was still amazed that God would give such a substantial purpose to such a significant sinner. I can only imagine a sense of relief that even though his life was coming to an end, the fulfillment of his life's purpose could not be erased.

Paul's life was one full of potential and preparation prior to his conversion in Acts 9. He was born in the capital Roman province of Tarsus, educated by the great Pharisee Gamaliel, enjoyed Roman citizenship, was a rising star in the Sanhedrin; the list could go on and on. He was without a doubt a man of influence and culture with a pedigree for success. But he was also, as we have already discovered, a man devoid of God-honoring purpose until his life was changed on the road to Damascus. Before that transformative moment, the theme of Paul's life was the law. After that moment, his life's theme was the grace of God.

The Meaning of Purpose

So the question becomes, What does the word *purpose* mean in Paul's life and in your own? The answer can be discovered in a private conversation between a disciple named Ananias and the Lord in Acts 9:15. Listen to how Jesus describes Paul's purpose to Ananias: "This man is my chosen instrument to take my name to Gentiles, kings, and Israelites." Now try to put yourself in Ananias's shoes. He was being told by the Lord in a vision to go and pray for the man who had made his reputation terrorizing followers of Jesus. No doubt it baffled and surely scared him, which is probably why he responded, "Lord, . . . I have heard from many people about this man, how much harm he has done to your saints in Jerusalem. And he has authority here from the chief priests to arrest all who call on your name" (Acts 9:13–14). Now I don't think Ananias is being disrespectful in any way;

I just think he is thoroughly confused and surprised by the Lord's request.

The beauty of God's purpose is that many times it will surpass human logic. It didn't make sense to Ananias that Saul—the murderous, Christian-killing Jew— who would later be known as Paul the apostle to the Gentiles, would be a "chosen instrument." God's grace always surprises not only the recipient but also those who observe such an event as well. The reason I suggest that Ananias meant no disrespect is that in the very next breath we witness him actively obeying the Word of the Lord.

God continually specializes in providing glorious purpose to individuals the rest of the world would consider undeserving. I hope as those who have been given grace and thus discovered our purpose, we always leave room in our thinking and imaginations for the unexpected. Furthermore, Ananias's example may serve as a reminder to us that our journeys should in fact intersect with dirty rotten sinners. After all, five minutes ago we were dirty rotten sinners who were then recipients of grace, and that may have confounded some unsuspecting onlookers.

We can see from this that there are three ingredients to the recipe of God's purpose. First, as discussed above, is the fact that God has chosen us to become followers of Jesus. Paul emphasized this when he wrote in Ephesians 1:4: "He chose us in him, before the foundation of the world, to be holy and blameless in love before him." Every Christian should have this compounding sense of gratitude for God because before we ever stepped foot on this planet He determined to love us. In a culture that is more image conscious than ever before, we are wired to earn others' love. But before we could edit out all the unwanted parts of ourselves, before we could select just the right pose and filter, God chose to love us. God, before the world was even created, looked down through time and history and said, "I choose you!" That is why I say again, the grace of God is that Jesus stepped onto the playground of our lives and said, "I choose you first."

Second, we are a chosen "instrument" or "vessel," which literally means "an instrument of choice."[1] The Lord, in his conversation with Ananias, uses the word *instrument* as a metaphor for Paul's pilgrimage.

There are two aspects to understanding the metaphor that our lives are instruments. First, we were chosen to be used *as* God's instruments. In other words, whatever type of instrument we may be exists to fulfill something God wants for His creation. A pilgrim is someone who aspires in his or her journey to be ever attentive to the desires of God, to be used by Him to accomplish His purposes. Second, God has created many different types of instruments to fulfill many different roles. Because in God's economy there are a multiplicity of instruments that fulfill a glorious array of assignments.

The third ingredient in God's recipe of purpose is that we were given a gift set so that we may fulfill an assignment. The Lord made Paul's assignment clear to Ananias: "To take my name to Gentiles, kings, and Israelites." So part of understanding purpose is grappling with the idea of completing tasks or objectives throughout our journey. And those assignments may change over time or with different stages of life. During one part of the journey, your assignment may be that of a student, but ten years down the road you may fulfill the role of artist or soldier or engineer or any number of things. Furthermore, the volume of assignments or tasks may vary depending on the stage of life as well.

For example, as I write this, I am currently fulfilling the assignment of husband and parent, organizational leader, preacher, and author. I am comfortable understanding that these assignments are graciously made possible because of God's goodness. In short, all pilgrims should know in the depths of their being that they were chosen and created to accomplish something for Jesus. Thus one of the greatest questions we can ask in our journeys is, "How has God gifted me, and how can I use that gift set to fulfill His wants for His creation?" Then spend your entire pilgrimage answering this question over and over again. Never stop asking that question, and you will never cease to live with purpose.

So let us close out our discussion on the meaning of purpose with three declarations. My prayer is that you will believe them and hold tightly to them as you journey onward.

A Declaration of Purpose

- Jesus stood on the playground of my life and said, "I choose you first!"
- God has uniquely created me with certain talents, abilities, and gifts.
- I will use my gift set to fulfill a multiplicity of assignments throughout my pilgrimage.

From Potential to Purpose

Potential has to do with showing signs of great promise and capability in the future. Adults frequently use the word when referring to young people and their futures. Or if someone seems to waste her life, you hear statements like, "She had so much unfulfilled potential."

You rarely hear the term applied to someone who is considered an adult. I think that is a shame and maybe even a little misguided. For example, Paul was certainly an adult before he became a follower of Jesus, realized his true purpose, and thus fulfilled much of his potential. I mention this only because I've met too many people who think it's too late to accomplish something for God with their lives. For anyone who may fall into that category, please know it is not too late. A pilgrimage enriched with purpose can begin today. God is asking us to journey and, as we journey, to represent the name of Jesus well.

And by the way, God hasn't chosen you because of what you could accomplish (i.e., potential); He has chosen you because of what Jesus has already accomplished (i.e., purpose). God has never stood on the playground of anyone's life and said, "I choose you first because of how talented you are or how much potential you possess." Such thinking is toxic and graceless! God chooses us because of His promise and His purpose for our lives. So let's not get too caught up in the notion of potential. Having a lot of potential is like having a screen full of emojis; there are a lot of them, and many will probably never get used, and some of them should never be used. Let's simplify it this way:

- Potential is about what you could do. Purpose is focused on what you should do.
- Potential is hypothetical. Purpose is hyper practical.
- Potential is about the unknown future. Purpose has to do with your life in the here and now.
- Potential revolves around your talents. Purpose revolves around living in light of God's promises with your talents.

In short, purpose is at the heart of pilgrimage. Now I'm not suggesting that potential is a bad word in any way. I'm just suggesting that the life of someone on a journey of following Jesus is enraptured with purpose. Purpose is the narrowing in and fulfillment of a specific task, role, or project for the glory of God. In short, it is doing what God placed you on this earth to do. You may have the potential to accomplish a lot of different things in life, but that doesn't necessarily mean you are purposed to do all those different things.

In his modern-day classic The Purpose Driven Life, pastor Rick Warren sums it up this way, "You were born by his purpose and for his purpose."[2] Paul wrote, "For everything, absolutely everything, above and below, visible and invisible . . . everything got started in him and finds its purpose in him" (Col. 1:16 MSG). Therefore, there is no way to know purpose apart from Jesus. That's why purpose must be understood along the lines of the aforementioned ingredients: Chosen—Instrument—Assignment(s).

Finally, let us journey onward with gratitude that Jesus chose us before we could ever choose Him. Let us journey onward operating with the gifts and talents He has given us. And let us journey onward fulfilling the various assignments that come our way. Then, and only then, do we discover an inward peace that Paul certainly experienced sitting in a Roman dungeon awaiting execution.

A Pilgrim's Purpose

Thus far we have seen the meaning of purpose, which begins with God's grace, and that the pilgrim's journey is consumed more with purpose than potential. Finally, I would like to paint a brief verbal picture of what it looks like to fulfill our ultimate purpose as followers of Jesus.

Paul wrote in 1 Corinthians 10:31, "So, whether you eat or drink, or whatever you do, do everything for the glory of God." So we were chosen, created to be God's instrument, and given an array of assignments throughout the journey. But ultimately it all comes down to, well, everything being done for God's glory.

To do something to the glory of God means that God is made obvious through the action. The pilgrim's ultimate purpose is to live in such a way that God is undeniable and obvious. And if that's the case, then there are certain shared characteristics of pilgrims wandering with purpose.

Pilgrims who live with purpose have identity, responsibility, belief, joy, and mission.

1. IDENTITY: Know that God took the broken pieces of his life and made it a masterpiece.[3]

> For we are God's masterpiece. He has cre-
> ated us anew in Christ Jesus, so we can do
> the good things he planned for us long ago.
> (Eph. 2:10 NLT)

2. RESPONSIBILITY: Bear the name of Jesus, and therefore understand the weight of responsibility that accompanies being a child of God.

3. BELIEF: Journey onward with a contagious courage and conviction.

In 1 Thessalonians 2 Paul describes how, after much abuse in Philippi, he and his companions came to preach in Thessalonica with boldness and courage:

> For you yourselves know, brothers and sis-
> ters, that our visit with you was not without
> result. On the contrary, after we had previ-
> ously suffered and were treated outrageously

in Philippi, as you know, we were embold-
ened by our God to speak the gospel of God
to you in spite of great opposition. (1 Thess.
2:1–2)

The great historian John Pollock demonstrates how the
courage and conviction of Paul and Silas were contagious
across demographic and cultural lines in the city:

> The courage and conviction of Paul and Silas
> bred further courage and conviction. Not
> only did converts assure fellow Jews that
> Jesus certainly was the Messiah, but they also
> broke out of their prejudices to tell pagan
> business acquaintances and the slaves who
> carried their goods from the docks that He
> was the Savior of everyone. Soon Jason's
> house, in a most un-Jewish way, became the
> center of a movement that spread like wild-
> fire across the city. In a few astonishing days
> "the church of the Thessalonians in God the
> Father and the Lord Jesus Christ" had more
> Greeks than Jews, both men and influential
> aristocratic women.[4]

4. JOY: Wander through this world with redemption
being the undeniable heart of the journey.

5. MISSION: Believe their pilgrimage should seek to fulfill God's desires.

The more we walk with Jesus, the more His purposes and
desires become our desires. This is probably what the fourth-
century church father Augustine meant when he wrote:
"Love God and do as you will."

Paul's Two Names

To close out this discussion on purpose, I want to bring our attention to the two names "the apostle to the Gentiles" applies to in Scripture: Saul and Paul. For most of my life, I thought "Saul" was simply his name prior to his conversion and the name "Paul" symbolized that he was in fact a new creation. Makes sense at first glance—new life equals new name. Saul was the sinner, and Paul was the apostle. The problem is that it just isn't true![5] He was actually a man with two names, which was common in that time period for someone with Hebrew heritage.

Without chasing too much of a rabbit, the name *Saul* reflects his Hebrew heritage, while *Paul* is his Greek name. Since Saul/Paul would be ministering primarily in Greco-Roman territories where his Roman citizenship would come in handy, beginning in Acts 13:13 he is henceforth referred to as Paul.

So what's the purpose in mentioning this little biblical tidbit that might only seem useful in a Bible trivia game of some sort? In Acts 13, Saul, who is also called Paul (v. 9), along with Barnabas, are beginning the first of three epic missionary journeys. In other words, Paul is his name as he begins what would end up being ten thousand miles of journeys expanding the movement of Christianity. The first time he is simply referred to this way, Luke writes, "Paul and his companions set sail from Paphos" (Acts 13:13). From this point forward, Paul's name is intrinsically bound to the advancement of the church.

Saul was a man of overwhelming potential, but Paul was a man who, with each passing day, was practically fulfilling and living his purpose—taking the gospel to the Gentile world. Paul was inevitably the name more suited for the pilgrimage God had in store.

I love the image that accompanies the first stand-alone "Paul" reference. Paul is in a boat with the wind in his sails, the sea breeze in his face, a handful of redeemed renegades at his side, and a glorious journey ahead.

This name shift teaches us that a pilgrim's purpose isn't discovered in the *doing* but rather in an inability to remain unresponsive to our new *being*. We get to wander through this world with our eyes wide open because we were once blind and now we see. Pilgrims cannot be stagnant in their life because it is contrary to their identity. We are not on a journey to accomplish something in an effort to please God enough that He may let us into the heaven country. No! We are on a pilgrimage because we have been made pilgrims. We were given sight so we can't help but discover creation with our own eyes. We were given life so breathing is a natural part of being alive. We walk and run and play because our muscles would atrophy if we didn't. We laugh because there is real, lasting joy in our formerly lifeless hearts. And we journey onward because the longing for eternity that exists within the depths of our souls is as real as the ground beneath our feet.

That is why I say, and will say again and again, pilgrims' purpose is to respond, with the tapestry that is their life, to the grace of God. And in that response, in those sacred, sweet moments, we know one thing clearer and louder than anything else: *This is my purpose.*

Three O'clock
Luke Alone Is with Me

There was once a life full of extraordinary stories. To hear of its twists and turns, its unlikely intersection with an eclectic group of people, would cause even the average person to wonder where fact would end and fiction would begin.

Edith Wilson Macefield's life was such a tale. And according to her, the narrative that made up her life actually happened. Here are just a few of the events and happenings that made Edith's life so extraordinary:

- She left home to work for the government at the age of fourteen.
- She ended up serving as an undercover British agent based in Germany during WWII.
- Her cover was music, which led her to play at functions where Adolf Hitler was present.
- She was found out to be a spy and placed in a Nazi concentration camp, where she helped thirteen Jewish children escape.

- At age eighteen Edith married a famous opera singer from Austria named Richard Tauber.
- While still legally married to Tauber, she also married a wealthy Yorkshire man who owned a plantation in Africa, where she lived for some time.
- She had a son with Tauber who died of spinal meningitis at age thirteen.
- For a period of time after the war, she ran an orphanage out of a castle in Cornwall, England, where she was also a sheep farmer.
- In her forties she moved home to Ballard, Washington, to care for her mother in her dying years.
- Edith married one more time to an Italian gentleman who died in a car accident on their honeymoon.
- She was an author and published a book titled *Where Yesterday Began* using her third husband's last name, Domilini, as her pen name.

There are so many more stories within the story of one Edith Wilson Macefield that time doesn't permit me to tell, like how she was cousins with the King of Swing, Barry Goodman, how she taught Mickey Rooney how to dance, or how she knew and even played with Tommy Dorsey, one of the greatest jazz musicians of all time. After her death handwritten notes were discovered in her house from several celebrities, including Katherine Hepburn. She had drawings hanging on a wall in her house specifically made for her from Academy Award winner Lionel Barrymore.

Toward the end of her life, this little old lady with white hair and hazel blue eyes only wanted one thing: to die in this little farmhouse, just outside of Seattle, Washington, as her mother had.

A shopping mall was being built in the area, and the developers desperately wanted Edith's property. She became something of a local hero because she continually refused any offer to sell the house, even when the price reached as high as $750,000. In the end they decided to build around the little 1,050 square-foot, 108-year-old farmhouse.

Barry Martin was the project supervisor for all the construction. Realizing that construction jobs often create a lot of noise and disruption, Barry made a habit of meeting all the neighbors and giving them his cell phone number if they ever had any questions. Through this practice Barry and Edith met for the first time. Neither of them realized the relational journey that had begun with a simple introduction. Soon thereafter Edith asked Barry to drive her to a hair appointment. Barry's involvement in Edith's life would evolve significantly and sometimes rapidly in the handful of years he knew her. What began as a trip to the hairdresser turned into being caregiver as Edith's body slowly began to deteriorate and shut down. With each setback Barry would step in. When Edith could no longer cook and clean her house, Barry made sure she had meals and the house was clean. When she lost the use of bodily functions, Barry cleaned her. When Edith fell, Barry was the one who rushed over to pick her up and get her to the couch. When she could no longer bathe herself or count her medicine, you guessed it, Barry. And before he left her each night, after he had set out her medicine, some cold water, and helped her to the bathroom one last time, he would kiss her on the forehead, tell her he loved her, and put in a CD of Richard Tauber. Occasionally, as he closed the front door, he would hear Edith say, "I love you too."

As Edith came to the end her life, facing her own dungeon called cancer, she knew one thing above all others: Barry Martin is here with me, and he will not leave me. In her own moments 'til midnight, she knew and experienced the beauty of love and enduring friendship. Barry Martin was Edith Wilson Macefield's friend until the end. I'm so grateful Barry decided to put Edith's life and their friendship into a book. As I turned through the pages of *Under One Roof: Lessons I Learned from a Tough Old Woman in a Little Old House* on a couple of recent flights, my eyes filled with tears on more than one occasion. It dawned on me as I came to the end of the book, I know about Edith's life because of Barry.[1] (On a completely unrelated note, I wonder how Edith would have felt about the Pixar movie *UP*, which is said to be loosely based on her determination to stay in her house.)

As the moments are ticking by and the final words of 2 Timothy are in clear view, Paul writes a short sentence that reads like a breath of fresh air: "Only Luke is with me" (2 Tim. 4:11). He goes on to articulate how so many others had departed, all in a letter being written to young Timothy whom he loved like a son. In his final letter Paul had clearly navigated the waters of loneliness and friendship, as will all pilgrims journeying home to the heaven country. Paul had enjoyed moments rich with community and brotherhood but was also familiar with the deafening silence of a dark dungeon. And when all was said and done, Luke was the one friend that stayed with him to the end.

When Paul finished writing 2 Timothy, simple logic would lead us to conclude that Luke delivered the correspondence. Just as we know about Edith's life because of Barry, so, in God's plan, Timothy and the rest of the world would read Paul's last letter because of Luke.

A Pilgrim's Friends

This little sentence about Luke communicates volumes concerning his friendship. That Paul mentions his co-laborer in the final moments of 2 Timothy certainly gives us evidence that as Paul sat in that dungeon with his pilgrimage coming to an end, the idea of friendship was close to his heart. Could it be that at three o'clock his thoughts would have focused on the friends he had known and the loneliness he had endured?

Reading 2 Timothy, and certainly other texts as well, one gets the sense that friendship mattered deeply to Paul. Luke was certainly one of his closest friends, having traveled with Paul many years (Acts 16:10; Col. 4:14; Phil. 24) and writing the book of Acts and the Gospel of Luke. Who could forget Barnabas, one of the first to believe in Paul's conversion and his true companion to so many cities and regions in the early days? And of course there was Timothy, whom Paul had befriended and become a spiritual father to from his teenage years until now.

Other friends and companions during his pilgrimage include Priscilla and Aquila, Silas, John Mark, and Titus. After a casual glance at Paul's friendships, the question becomes, What can these individuals teach us about the value and role of friendship?

Friends Prioritize Presence over Productivity

As Paul came to the end of his journey, only Luke was with him. Everyone else had left or even abandoned him for one reason or another. Some may have left because they felt there was nothing more they could do for Paul by remaining in Rome. Paul uses strong language when describing how his fellow-laborer Demas had left him (2 Tim. 4:10.) The Greek word he uses means "to abandon, desert, leave in straits, leave helpless, leave in the lurch, let one down."[2] Paul does not mince words when describing Demas's behavior.

Others may have wanted to pursue other ministry assignments, some of which may have even come from Paul. But through it all Luke remained present. And his presence teaches us something incredibly insightful regarding friendship: *real friends value being with over doing for.*

We live in a world where the term *friend* doesn't mean what it used to mean. So much of our "friendships" are really just acquaintances or associations. We have stuff in common with that person, or we follow each other on Instagram. We sit next to that person at school or that fellow mom who drives a super-cool gray minivan at your kid's practice. But just because the term has been watered down a bit does not mean that there is not an authentic notion of friendship that still remains and is still worth cultivating.

The first and possibly greatest quality, certainly because of the challenges we face in our culture, is the willingness to be present. A true friend physically shows up, as opposed to sending some love on social media or shooting a text message with a well-thought-out GIF. You can't be present from a distance, any more than you can engage with all five senses from afar. While this is possibly the greatest quality, herein also lies the secret of friendship. True friends are willing to simply show up.

Friends that prioritize being present over any other kind of productivity are the friends that journey with you. They are fellow pilgrims wandering their way home. These friends don't stand on the sideline of your path or journey and cheer you on. Rather they are shoulder to shoulder with you, sweating and exerting themselves right beside you. They don't need to shout out words of encouragement because they are close enough to whisper and you would hear. True friends help bear your burden, cry with you, laugh with you, and may even bleed alongside you. While each pilgrim personally responds to the calling of God, no pilgrim journeys alone. And although each pilgrim will get out of the boat and will step their own two feet in the heaven country, no pilgrim was in the boat alone.

Friends Don't Have to Qualify to Receive Quality

Living in a world that has watered down the definition of friendship has unfortunately produced a culture of fakeness, posturing, and an overconcern with appearance. We spend so much of our time positioning how we look on social media, always trying to crop out the unwanted and use just the right filter. We have become experts at distorting what was put into the image or what we would like it to be. Sadly this has affected our approach to friendships. While few of us would say it out loud, we certainly think in terms of what people can offer us before we can be friends with them. We want our associations to improve our appearance.

I'm afraid I live in a world where friendship has been reduced to branding and brand control. But this should not be true of pilgrims making their way home.

In the end Paul could offer Luke nothing. In fact, Luke, a doctor, would have offered medical assistance when allowed by the Roman guards. Theirs was a friendship that didn't require Paul to qualify for Luke to remain and endure as his friend. Luke gave his best to Paul at a time when Paul could give him nothing in return. And this could be said of Timothy and Paul's relationship as well. Timothy didn't have to live up to some expectation for their friendship to endure.

The evidence that we have is to the contrary. Paul loved Timothy, weaknesses and all. The point here is clear: they were pilgrims, bound together vocationally by a common calling, resolved to love each other well, as friends should always do.

C. S. Lewis wrote a book toward the end of his life entitled *The Four Loves*. In it he studies the four main Greek words for love and expounds on their meanings. One of the four loves is *phileo* or friendship love. To give you an example of how this word can be used, *Philadelphia* is a combination of the two Greek words for love (*phileo*) and brother (*adelphos*), thus giving it the nickname "The City of Brotherly Love." Of this friendship love Lewis wrote:

> Friendship is something that raised us almost above humanity. This love, free from instinct, free from all duties but those which love has freely assumed, almost wholly free from jealousy, and free without qualification from the need to be needed, is eminently spiritual. It is the sort of love one can imagine between angels.[3]

Friendship love doesn't demand that you qualify for my love before I grant it; rather, it cares freely and completely. Neither is this type of love looking for opportunity for any kind of advancement or improvement of status. No, a friend's love is that of a traveling companion, an image well suited for any discussion on Paul. Friendship love cares without being competitive, critiques without being critical, meets needs without ever keeping a tab, and carries onward without comparison. True friends come alongside for a season or the better part of the journey, and they care for our well-being as much as their own. A friend is a fellow wanderer who, likewise, is simply going home.

Friends Seek to Understand before Being Understood

At the beginning of Paul's last letter, he spent several verses encouraging young Timothy in the faith. Timothy was Paul's most trusted and loyal co-laborer for the gospel. Furthermore, he viewed him as a son, which is never more clearly demonstrated than in Philippians 2:19–22:

> Now I hope in the Lord Jesus to send Timothy to you soon so that I too may be encouraged by news about you. For I have no one else like-minded who will genuinely care about your interests; all seek their own interests, not those of Jesus Christ. But you know his proven character, because he has served with me in the gospel ministry like a son with a father.

Part of Paul's encouragement to Timothy was to recognize his emotional struggles. We see this when he writes of "remembering your tears" (2 Tim. 1:4). He began his correspondence by essentially saying, "Hey buddy, I know it was really tough on you the last time we had to say good-bye to each other. I know a lot of tears were shed. I think of you like a son and want you to know I haven't forgotten how hard this is on you. Hang in there, man, because soon we will be together and our hearts will be full of joy again."

What comfort it must have brought to Timothy that his father in the ministry, the man he looked up to more than any other, remembered the emotional toil all this was taking on him. Before Paul would share the incredible and life-changing content that would make up the bulk of the letter, he wanted this young man to know he was understood. Paul sought to understand Timothy before helping Timothy understand a message.

When I was a boy, someone told me an old adage: "Boy, God gave you two ears and one mouth, so you should listen twice as much as you speak." While friends are fellow pilgrims wandering through this broken world, remember that every pilgrim is different and every pilgrimage poses its unique set of challenges. A friend realizes this and thus seeks to understand context, recent events, and trials. In other words, a friend exercising *phileo* makes understanding a fellow pilgrim the utmost priority. Friends are constantly mastering the art of listening and asking the right questions. In short, real friends are deeply concerned with knowing the person they are journeying with.

The idea of understanding before being understood has been, in large measure, lost on us in a culture of competing voices. It seems whoever speaks first, loudest, and longest, or is the most bombastic and dogmatic, gets heard the most. But I often wonder if filling the air with a lot of hot air accomplishes anything. I wonder if we are all drowning in a sea of noise of our own making. I wonder how different our relationships and friendships would be if we spent more time listening, understanding, and really processing what we heard. Maybe we've just gotten things a bit twisted. Could it be that we fill the air because we think the point is to be heard? But what if the purpose wasn't to be heard but rather to be known and to know. Knowing and being known begins with truly prioritizing understanding before being understood.

Friends Are Quick to Set Aside Self in Order to Sacrifice

Jesus said in John 15:13, "No one has greater love than this: to lay down his life for his friends." Paul obviously took this to heart. Paul spent the better part of thirty years and ten thousand miles with like-minded men willing to set aside earthly comfort. They were willing to sacrifice everything for gospel advancement but also for one another. And they walked into this with their eyes wide open. They knew they would be trading the safety of home for the dangers of the road, a warm bed for a mat in the dirt, and four walls and a roof for nights chained to the walls of a dungeon. Each man had to know the journey ahead could mean their demise. This calling, this camaraderie, would most likely end with violence.

Each of us—from the moment of birth—immediately needs a family. Paul alone was blinded on that Damascus road on his way to stamp out Christianity, but when he was made spiritually new or born again, he needed a spiritual family. And it couldn't be just some folks that made for good conversation around the fire at night. No, he needed a handful of radicals like himself. He needed some Jesus freaks, some redeemed renegades. Those who were willing to get dirt underneath their fingernails and weren't afraid to put some blood in the dirt. Men like Barnabas.

The first time we met Barnabas he had just sold his property and donated the money to the apostles to be used for the Christian community. From our introduction to him in Scripture, we see a willingness to sacrifice earthly comfort for the cause of Christ.

Yes, Barnabas sacrificed his resources for the cause (Acts 4:36–37), but he sacrificed a portion of his life to serve with Paul. It would be difficult to overestimate his influence in the early days of Paul's pilgrimage. Barnabas vouched for Paul with doubting Jewish Christians. According to Acts 9:27, he was the one who introduced Paul to Jesus' disciples in Jerusalem: "Barnabas, however, took him and brought him to the apostles and explained to them how Saul had seen the Lord on the road and that the Lord had talked to him, and how in Damascus he had spoken boldly in the name of Jesus." Barnabas was growing in favor and influence with the church in Jerusalem because he was "a good man, full of the Holy Spirit and of faith" (Acts 11:24). They had sent him to minister in the prominent city of Antioch, and after he had been there for some time, "he went to Tarsus to search for Saul, and when he found him he brought him to Antioch. For a whole year they met with the church and taught large numbers. The disciples were first called Christians at Antioch" (Acts 11:25–26).

Both Paul and Barnabas were later commissioned by the church at Antioch to take the gospel to the Gentiles, which would be the first of three missionary journeys. Even though the two would eventually part ways over a disagreement concerning Barnabas's cousin John Mark, the momentum of the movement only continued to pick up steam.

Barnabas saw something in Paul that no one else seemed to recognize. He believed in Paul when no one else would. He vouched for him to the men who had followed Jesus so closely. One has to wonder whether Paul would ever have been able to write the words "Only Luke is with me" (2 Tim. 4:11) if years earlier Barnabas hadn't been there for him. He decided on his own to go to Paul's hometown of Tarsus and bring him into the movement. Through Barnabas's sacrifice of money, reputation, time, and energy, he helped launch the greatest leader the church has ever seen. Barnabas viewed his sacrifice as a natural expression of service for the movement of Christianity that continues to change the world today.

One Friendship Can Change the World

In the end we are always willing to sacrifice for what truly matters. It is evident from Barnabas's sacrifice that wandering with Paul was definitely a worthwhile endeavor. It is not an exaggeration to say that Barnabas changed the world through one friendship. It's amazing to think that one person, seeing God at work in another, then sacrificing in service and friendship to that individual, can have a ripple effect that surpasses anyone's expectations! True friends don't see sacrifice as an interruption to a relationship but rather as an ingredient.

Just as Barry was a friend to Edith in helping her live and die with dignity, so Paul's friends helped him journey onward and finish his race well. In one sense that's what friendship is all about. We exist not for ourselves but to know and be known, to help fellow sojourners journey well so they may finish well and so we can all meet in paradise for an everlasting party. Maybe that's why God gave us the gift of friendship—because it's essential to the pilgrimage.

Many believe Barry and Edith's friendship inspired the movie UP. In the years that followed Edith's death, the little farmhouse has come to be known as "The UP House" and stands as a memorial to the determination of a feisty old lady in a little old house. But every time I see the picture of that little house surrounded on three sides by massive concrete walls, I see a memorial to friendship. I see the place where two people forged an unlikely bond.

Adventure is out there! But it's not what you might have initially thought. The adventure is knowing and being known, it's journeying onward with fellow pilgrims. Everyone journeys; no one should journey alone. To do so would be to miss out on so much of the adventure that is our pilgrimage.

Four O'clock
Head in the Clouds

By four o'clock Paul knew his pilgrimage was soon coming to an end. To stay with the analogy in Hebrews 11:13, the shoreline of his celestial destination was in clearer view than ever before. Paul now desired a better place—a heavenly one (Heb. 11:16). And yet as the heaven country seemed just around the bend, one idea could easily have consumed his thoughts on this late afternoon hour: thinking about heaven is what has guided the duration of his pilgrimage. The reason Paul, the pilgrim, was able to stay so focused on journeying well here on Earth was because he had so fully embraced a heavenly mind-set.

He addressed this notion of a heavenly mind-set when writing to the people of Colossae. In this letter Paul was writing to people whom he had never met personally but who had most likely heard about and held a deep respect for his leadership. He was communicating Christ in a city where the climate was growing cold toward true Christianity and warm toward heretical teaching. It might even be safe to characterize the culture of Colossae as growing more and more spiritual yet less and less Christian. He was writing to Christ followers who probably met in houses weekly and whose faith was under attack. In this environment Paul wrote concerning the centrality of Christ in all things and the manner in which a Christian should live and believe.

Paul, like all pilgrims, was a child of two worlds. He was passing through a world broken by sin while his truest citizenship belonged to a world where God's desired will was constantly on full display. He kept his head in the clouds, so to speak, as he walked a path littered with both obstacles and opportunities. A heavenly mind-set in the final hours of his life was nothing new, for Paul had lived with an eye on heaven and an eye on Earth for years now.

A Pilgrim's Mentality

> . . . begins with fully embracing heaven's idea for our lives.

When Paul wrote about this notion of a heavenly mind-set (Col. 3:1–4)—living with your head in the clouds—he did so with emphasis. Paul was a man acutely aware of the grace of Jesus in the present moment. He knew, and made crystal clear, that before we could reach up to heaven, heaven reached down to us. The entire emphasis of the first four verses has to do with how heaven has made salvation possible on Earth. Follow this sequence:

- "You have been raised to new life with Christ,"
- So "set your sights on the realities of heaven,"
- "You died to this life,"

- "And your real life is hidden with Christ in God."
- Thus, "Christ . . . is your life." (Col. 3:1–4 NLT)

In one sense Paul's logic here leaves us with a sacred paradox: *to live effectively on Earth I must fully embrace heaven's idea for my life.* This is what Paul means when he says to "set your sights on the realities of heaven" and to "think about the things of heaven" (Col. 3:1–2 NLT). Heaven has purchased our salvation; therefore, our response should be to embrace heaven's idea for our lives. Paul is teaching us that the price our salvation cost heaven should be the filter for our mind-set in this journey.

C. S. Lewis brilliantly expressed this idea in his classic work *Mere Christianity* when he wrote:

> A continual looking forward to the eternal world is not (as some modern people think) a form of escapism or wishful thinking, but one of the things a Christian is meant to do. It does not mean that we are to leave the present world as it is. If you read history you will find that the Christians who did most for the present world were just those who thought most of the next. The Apostles themselves, who set on foot the conversion of the Roman Empire, the great men who built up the Middle Ages, the English Evangelicals who abolished the Slave Trade, all left their mark on Earth, precisely because their minds were occupied with heaven. It is since Christians have largely ceased to think of the other world that they have become so ineffective

in this. Aim at Heaven and you will get Earth "thrown in"; aim at Earth and you will get neither.[1]

We are to live with this sort of heavenly mind-set. Our pilgrimage has a destination, and focusing on the destination empowers us to be helpful along the way. The question then becomes, What does it really look like to journey with a heavenly mind-set, to allow this idea to determine how we think? A heavenly mind-set means:

- We have a new identity: we have been raised to new life.
- We have a new perspective: we must set our sights on the realities of heaven.
- We have a new understanding of success and purpose: Christ is our life. We will share in all His glory.

In short, people of faith have no other option than to think differently from those who see this world as their home. For the pilgrim, heaven has "come a-calling" and thus changed not only our hearts but our heads as well. We keep our head in the clouds because we don't want our feet to get too comfortable on the ground. Heaven consumes our thoughts because we don't want to get too comfortable with our present surroundings. Heaven captures our imagination because we long to go there, and because heaven has changed us, we know that one glad morning we will arrive on the shores of glory.

Plato defined thinking as "the talking of the soul with itself." The writer of Proverbs 23:7 put it this way, "As he thinks in his heart, so is he" (NKJV). Both Plato and the writer of Proverbs help us understand that when we are intentional with our thoughts, it affects our whole being and thus determines how we live.

The great reformer John Calvin also wrestled with this notion of heavenly thinking:

> But if we ought to think of nothing but of what is heavenly, because Christ is in heaven, how much less becoming were it to seek Christ upon the earth. Let us therefore bear in mind that that is a true and holy thinking as to Christ, which forthwith bears us up into heaven, that we may there adore him, and that our minds may dwell with him.[2]

Heavenly thinking causes me to live in a state of adoration for Jesus. This type of thinking determines the type of journey we will lead and the type of life we will live. Those who keep their heads in the clouds will keep their eyes on Jesus, and thus, their hearts will be full of reverence, worship, and gratitude. Those who live with their heads in the clouds know not only how to live well but also how to love well. So I ask you, Is there a better way to wander through this world?

. . . knows the war with self has been won and can continue to be won

There are some pretty amazing and significant impacts heavenly mind-set has on our earthly journey. One is, of course, the idea of winning the war with the flesh, which Paul writes about in Colossians 3:5–9. He writes about the sins of the flesh with a profound intensity, quickly shifting from the positive of heavenly thinking to the negative concerning putting sin to death in our lives.

The order here is vitally important. Paul does not tell us to put sin to death and then embrace heaven but rather to embrace heaven and then put sin to death. It is a great reminder that *true victory comes from above*. If we are in Christ, we have the power to win the war with self because God in salvation has broken the power of evil in our lives. In other words, the way we rise above our sins is by embracing heaven's idea for our lives.

Nevertheless, Paul uses strong language to address our sin when he writes, "put to death" (Col. 3:5) and "put off all these" (Col. 3:8 NKJV). As believers, we have the power to reject evil and fleshly desires. The phrase "to put to death" could be translated "to mortify" and is used to speak of putting to death or treating something as dead.[3] So we should live as if the old ways motivated by selfish and fleshly desire are dead to us.

The Message articulates it this way: "And that means killing off everything connected with that way of death" (Col. 3:5 MSG). And at this point Paul is specific and relevant, both then and now, by providing a list that focuses on a wide assortment of sins or offenses.

- "Sexual immorality" and "impurity" meaning any sexual activity outside of marriage. The word for "sexual immorality" in the Greek is *porneia*, which means "illicit sexual behavior in general." This is where we get the word for *porn* or *pornography*. The term for *impurity* means "uncleanness in a moral sense, the impurity of lustful, luxurious, profligate living."[4] These two phrases are all-encompassing, covering everything from sex to sexting, from suggestive selfies to suggestive clothing.

- "Lust" and "evil desire" speak to "depraved passion" and "wicked cravings."[5] These two words together could be understood as sinful lust. Like the first two items on Paul's list, these describe a wide range of activity: pornography, whether in movies, on social media, or on explicit porn sites; fantasizing about sexual images or someone in "real life." These words could also be pointing to a range of other sins including lust for power, fame, money, or possessions.

- "Greed," which is the idea of having more and wanting more. More what, we may ask? Well, you name it, *more* could refer to money, sex, or power, but in any case it is a vacuum that cannot be filled. Sin never fills and never satisfies but rather creates a bigger space to be filled. Sin always decays the body and the soul, leaving us unsatisfied and wanting more. This may be why Paul describes greed as an idol or a god in someone's life because the desire for more is a form of idolatrous worship.

- "Anger," "wrath" or rage, "malice," and "slander": These four words paint a picture of a hateful attitude and potential outbursts toward others. The word for *anger* describes habitual attitudes, while wrath or rage refers to the sudden outburst of anger.[6] The word for *malice* has to do with an attitude of ill will toward a person. Warren Wiersbe writes, "If we have malice toward a person, we are sad when he is successful, and we rejoice when he has trouble. This is sinful."[7] We can have a hateful attitude toward those we know personally and/or toward those we have never met. Slander is simply any kind of speech meant to tear someone down.

- "Filthy language": This type of language is the result of anger, rage, malice, and slander and refers to any type of abusive speech. Paul writes elsewhere, "Let there be no filthiness nor foolish talk nor crude joking, which are out of place, but instead let there be thanksgiving" (Eph. 5:4 ESV). It is important to see certain types of language as contrary to heavenly conduct. Imagine you are walking down the streets of heaven enjoying the presence of Jesus and all the saints living in eternal and perfect harmony. Let's say along the way you stop and have a few conversations or meet up with some people for a cup of coffee and good conversation. During the course of that conversation at the corner café just steps off a golden street, could you ever imagine using some of the slang we use now? You know the words that aren't official curse words but rather substitute words so we can feel better about ourselves after using them? And there is the point when we embrace heaven, we likewise begin to live as if those words are no longer available to us.

- "Do not lie": To lie is to misrepresent God and imitate Satan who is the father of lies (John 8:44). In fact, Titus 1:2 teaches that God cannot tell a lie. Paul is teaching us that lying is the type of talk and activity the old self, who wasn't a Christ follower, would do. Someone made new in Christ is trustworthy through and through, and this is evident in her speech. In other words, Christians should be the most believable and trustworthy people on the planet.

What are we to make of such an extensive, yet specific, list? Years ago I used to work at a lumberyard during the summers and after school. It was an eye-opening experience to say the least. Some of the guys who worked the yard did so because they were on work release from jail. Others were just trying to make ends meet while they looked for better employment. Some were guys who had made a career of it. If you've never had the opportunity of frequenting such an establishment, you're not missing out on too much.

A lumberyard's purpose is to sell the necessary products for the construction of homes, so basically every kind of wood product, siding, shingles, etc., is there. The lumberyard is also, at first glance, a chaotic scene of forklifts moving stacks of lumber, people running every which direction filling orders and keeping the yard clean. But if the foreman knows what he is doing, the yard functions well.

I'll never forget our yard foreman, a man who appeared to have spent much of his time using drugs. Even though he was often impaired on the job, there was always a quick wit about him. Each morning, shortly after we had all clocked in, he would gather his employees and hand out assignments. Each of these "assignment meetings" ended with the same admonition. The foreman would pause, clear his throat, and say, "Boys, all of you is just one step away from stupid; don't take that step today and we'll all be OK!"

After I graduated from high school, went to college and seminary, got married, had kids, and have now run an organization for many years, the yard foreman's wisdom is still in my head. And I think for good reason.

Even though Christ through the cross has broken the power of sin over our lives, and even though we can put to death the old ways, the old self never fully dies in this life. The flesh, the old man, whatever name we call it by, still exists. In fact, the flesh has an insatiable appetite. It can be fed all day long and still be hungry.

As I read through Paul's list of inward and outward sins, I am reminded of just how easily I can fall back into the old ways. I am reminded of Christ's sufficiency and that I must daily put to death that which leads to death. I must live as if sin isn't even an option, not because of some list but because heaven has made a way for me to be redeemed. Finally, this list reminds me that I must have a personal and genuine faith that is my own because who I am on the inside will eventually manifest itself on the outside.

So after all these years, the yard foreman is still correct, at least for me. I am always one step away from stupid. Thank goodness for what Paul writes about next.

. . . is that of someone made "new" who never grows old

The pilgrim's mind-set begins with embracing heaven's idea for our lives, which allows us to win the battle we all face with our flesh and the old man. Now Paul turns his attention to putting on the new man. Paul writes in Colossians 3:10–11, "Put on the new self. You are being renewed in knowledge according to the image of your Creator. In Christ there is not Greek and Jew, circumcision and uncircumcision, barbarian, Scythian, slave and free; but Christ is all and in all." The great truth of these verses is that we have been made NEW! Elsewhere he writes, "If anyone is in Christ, he is a new creation; the old has passed away, and see, the new has come!" (2 Cor. 5:17).

The Greek language has two words for *new*. The first is *neos* meaning "new in time," and the second is *kainos* meaning "new in quality."[8] Both of these terms help us understand what it means to "put on the new self."

First, when we cross the line of faith, we are made new in Christ Jesus once and for all. And part of the beauty and miracle of God's grace is that we will never become old in Christ! Think about that, we are forever new creations, new men and women in Jesus: "Because of the LORD's faithful love we do not perish, for his mercies never end. They are new every morning; great is your faithfulness!" (Lam. 3:22–23). Putting off the old man and putting on the new man is a once-and-for-all action that determines my daily status in the journey. Whether I've been wandering on my way home for five minutes or fifty years, I am new in Christ.

Second, once we have been made new in Christ, we are also continually renewed as we grow in our faith. The more we get to know Jesus, the more we become like Jesus. Therefore, the goal of someone who has been made new is to live new, as he or she gets to know Jesus more.

The pilgrim's mind-set is that he or she gets to journey homeward knowing that God has kissed every day with His presence. We journey as those who have been made new this moment and every future moment through Christ's sufficiency. We journey as those who have been made new both in time and in quality. In other words, I am made new on every calendar date from this point forward, and I am new through and through in my soul and being.

And, of course, in typical all-encompassing fashion, Paul demonstrates how being made new doesn't create new division but rather causes old division to disappear. This is an invitation to join the greatest movement by going on the most important pilgrimage history has ever known. The new life heaven has made possible causes all other distinguishing characteristics to take a back seat.

I think we can all agree that we live in a world of distinctions and division: republican/democrat, hipster/skater, athlete/mathlete, white/black, American/Iranian, Baptist/Methodist. But God bids you to come to Jesus and start a journey. Then we can discover something beautiful and mesmerizing, something no other movement has ever accomplished: *in Jesus there is no distinction because in Jesus distinctions disappear:*

- There is no nationality: *neither Greek nor Jew.*
- There are no former religious differences: *neither circumcision nor uncircumcision.*
- There is no cultural divide: *barbarian, Scythian.*
- There is no upper class or lower class: *slave, free.*

In Jesus we are all new and being conformed more and more into the image of our Creator. In Jesus we are one, we are new, because hallelujah and amen, "Christ is all and in all."

Final Thoughts on Having Our Heads in the Clouds

The world is full of people whose thoughts are consumed with the temporal. In reality we are all guilty of it to one extent or another. We fixate on the latest drama in the political arena, we are consumed with the so-called reality of entertainment and entertainers, or we spend what looks a little too much like cyber-stalking amount of time focusing on the lives of those in close proximity. The point is that if we aren't careful, our brains will gobble up the latest drama, gossip, or comings and goings on stuff that ultimately doesn't matter. It's just cotton candy. It tastes good in the moment but dissolves so quickly that we have to reach into the bag with our sticky fingers for more. It's an evergreen temptation of humanity to fixate forever on the ultimately unimportant.

But when we put off the old man and put on the new, we change the way we think. We realize that redemption didn't begin on a hill far, far away; it started in heaven before the foundations of the world. If Paul demonstrates anything, it's that heaven's purpose can stop you in your tracks, change your life here and now, and replace a pointless existence with an adventure of epic proportions.

And because our salvation started in heaven, we long to go there. It's like there is now a heavenly instinct woven into the fabric of our thinking and feeling. Like a sea turtle who returns to the same beach year after year to lay her eggs or the salmon who swims up a particular stream to do the same, something in us now stirs us onward to the place where all this began.

We could use a few more people in this world who have their heads in the clouds. I heard someone say once, "That person is so heavenly minded, he is no earthly good." That's ridiculous! The greatest good one can have on Earth is when he or she has a heavenly mind-set.

A heavenly mind-set simplifies life.

A heavenly mind-set helps you attribute
value to what truly matters.

A heavenly mind-set keeps the troubles
of this world in perspective.

A heavenly mind-set reminds
you every day of grace.

A heavenly mind-set reminds
others of grace.

So go on, pilgrim, with your thoughts on heaven and your feet firmly on the ground. Keep going and journey onward, wander forward with your head in the clouds. Know it's OK to be different and think differently; know that you *are* different. While the world around you is consumed, with sticky fingers and an empty stomach, you think contrary to the tide of common thought, so your life is a living reminder of an altogether different and infinitely better path. Because your head is in the clouds, your journey points others to the home that God has made possible for all who look up and embrace heaven's idea for their lives, look inward and continually win the war with self, and look forward, living everyday like you've been made new.

Five O'clock
Getting Dressed with Grace

I don't like to get dressed up. I'm sure a well-intended member of some generation before my time would call me lazy. But for me, wearing a suit or even tucking in a shirt seems both ornate and poor time management. On any given day, and whenever I can get by with it, I'm jeans-and-T-shirt'n it all the way. In fact, it's so bad that when Chris and I got married, I didn't even know how to tie a tie. On our honeymoon we set sail on a cruise ship to the Caribbean. On the last evening dinner gathering, we were supposed to get dressed up in what I can only describe as "big church clothes." While my new wife was getting ready for the evening, putting on a beautiful dress, makeup, and smell-good stuff, I was standing in front of a mirror with a dress shirt on and staring at the tie in my hand not having the faintest idea how to even begin.

I hadn't told her that I didn't know how to tie a tie, and in that moment I didn't want to admit it. She looked like something that just stepped out of a dream, and here I am feeling like the village idiot. To cover for my embarrassment, I told her I was going to step out for a few minutes and would be right back. Being the newlyweds that we were, she continued with her preparations in front of the mirror and just smiled saying in carefree voice, "OK, see you in a few!"

So here I am walking down the hall, tie in hand, and not a clue how to resolve my dilemma. I don't know what I was thinking, but at that moment an older gentleman walked by heading to his cabin. I nodded and said hello, and he nodded back and responded the same. After he passed me and when he was a considerable distance down the hall, I turned around suddenly and blurted out, "Hey man, do you mind if I ask you a question?" He looked up a bit surprised, shrugged his shoulders, and said, "Sure." By this time I was walking in his direction, and when I was within "inside voice" distance, I explained, "I'm on my honeymoon, and my wife is almost ready to go to dinner. Tonight is the night we are supposed to get really dressed up, and she looks amazing. I've done my best to dress appropriately, but—and here is my dilemma—I don't know how to tie a tie!"

At this moment I lifted my hand in his direction with the tie draped over my palm like I was making an offering out of it. The gentleman—several years my senior—looked up at me. He was a short man with a stocky build. He smiled—the kind of smile someone uses when he feels sorry for someone else. I knew in that moment that he pitied me, and I was hoping to hear some kind words.

His response was comforting but at the same time created another dilemma: "Well son, I certainly know how to tie a tie, but you and I are different measurements. I can't tie the tie on me and give it to you because you're tall. And I can't reach up and tie it on you because I can't tie a tie backwards." He took a deep breath and looked me up and down. I could tell he had an idea in his head but wasn't sure he wanted to verbalize it. "Follow me," he then said hesitantly.

We walked a few more steps, and he opened the door to his cabin. *Great*, I thought, *but how are we going to do this?* Once the door shut behind us, he said, "Come stand next to the bed and face the mirror." I think I heard him mutter under his voice saying that if his wife walked in at this moment, boy would she get a good laugh. So there I am standing at the end of his bed facing the mirror. He then stands on the end of his bed and begins to tie my tie so that I could look nice for my wife on our first formal meal as husband and wife. When he finished, this spry short guy jumped down and looked me over again, making sure everything was in its proper place.

At this point we did what only two grown men who are complete strangers can do after such an ordeal. We laughed, and I mean laughed loud—the type of belly laugh you feel in your gut. Shortly thereafter I expressed my gratitude and returned to my room. When I walked in, my wife said, "Well, don't you look spiffy in your coat and tie!"

You know, I have to admit that it was kind of nice to be fully and appropriately dressed for our dinner date. And, with a certain amount of reluctance, I have found a small measure of satisfaction in wearing a suit when the occasion calls for it. I think we would all admit that something just feels right when you are dressed properly for an occasion.

As pilgrims making our way to the home country, we put on a certain spiritual attire when we put off the old man. It is safe to say that Paul lived and died fully dressed in what we will call "the wardrobe of grace."

He teaches us in Colossians 3:12–14 that because we are chosen by God, we are already "holy and dearly beloved." Therefore we clothe ourselves with these virtues:

> compassion, kindness, humility, gentleness,
> and patience, bearing with one another
> and forgiving one another if anyone has a

> grievance against another. Just as the Lord
> has forgiven you, so you are also to forgive.
> Above all, put on love, which is the perfect
> bond of unity.

His language stirs up the image of a piece of apparel or an item of clothing that goes together to make up an outfit—a wardrobe of grace. We will focus on these qualities, which in many ways, paint for us a picture of the spiritual attire that reveals one undeniable truth: we are loved and have been chosen by God, and our lives are "hidden with Christ in God" (Col. 3:3).

For Paul it is now five o'clock, and there is no doubt that the central theme of Colossians ran through his thoughts: *Christ is enough.* That Christ is enough, which speaks to his sufficiency and supremacy, means that in repenting and believing in Jesus we become characterized by and begin to live by His grace. In the last chapter we looked at putting off the old and having our lives hidden with Christ in God. Now we get to investigate the specifics of what we put on when we believe.

Jesus and His gospel, in its divine power, works this putting off and putting on. In other words, we are never spiritually naked because the moment we repented and believed, Jesus transformed us from the rags of our old selves to clothing us in the richness of His grace. Our text answers exactly what we put on—all that encompasses the wardrobe of grace and how that affects the way we live. With death imminently approaching and the Roman sun just beginning to set, Paul would have been comforted by the fact that he was fully clothed in the richness of God's grace. In short, no matter the cruel intentions of his captors and the extent to which he would be once again tortured before his death, Paul would die fully dressed in God's grace.

And just as Paul would die fully clothed in Christ's richness, so we wander arrayed with the same wardrobe. God not only calls us to journey home, but He provides for us all that is necessary to travel well. Without a doubt, God has clothed the pilgrim for the journey

A Pilgrim's Attire: The Wardrobe of Grace

Heartfelt Compassion: How We Feel toward Others

The first item of clothing gets straight to the heart of the matter. We are to care and feel deeply toward others as we journey. This phrase could also be translated "tender mercies" or even "bowels of mercy." Yikes! How are the bowels in any way connected to the notion of compassion?!

Well, to the ancient Greek poets, "the bowels were regarded as the seat of the more violent passions, such as anger and love: but by the Hebrews as the seat of the tenderer affections, especially kindness, benevolence, compassion, hence, our *heart*, tender mercies, affections."[1] So if you were to go back a couple of thousand years, people wouldn't cringe at a phrase that included "bowels" and "mercy." For them, the idea of tender emotions was connected with the stirring of internal physical organs.[2]

Think about it this way. Paul was talking about feeling mercy or care as deeply as one could; hence we get the phrase "heartfelt compassion." For our purposes a Christian's concern for others should run deep. But whom should we care about? Where should such heartfelt concern be directed?

To answer this question, we must go back to when Jesus Himself used this term. In Luke 10:25–37, Jesus told a Jewish audience the story of a good Samaritan in response to a lawyer's question concerning eternal life. Basically a normal, everyday Joe is walking down a road from Jerusalem to Jericho. Unbeknown to him, a gang of bandits was patiently waiting for a victim they could beat senseless, steal from, and leave dying in the ditch on the side of the road. With the aftermath of their victim bleeding out and dying, both an associate priest and a priest passed the dying man, never offering any assistance. Then Jesus said, "But a Samaritan on his journey came up to him, and when he saw the man, he had compassion" (v. 33). What happens next is a marvelous visual of heartfelt compassion:

> When he saw the man's condition, his heart went out to him. He gave him first aid, disinfecting and bandaging his wounds. Then he lifted him onto his donkey, led him to an inn, and made him comfortable. In the morning he took out two silver coins and gave them to the innkeeper, saying, "Take good care of him. If it costs any more, put it on my bill—I'll pay you on my way back." (Luke 10:33–35 MSG)

The Samaritan, who is the most Christlike character in the story, completely cared for the dying man. He didn't just observe his pain; he felt his pain. He didn't send help; he became the help the dying man needed. He didn't set a limit on his assistance; he put the entire tab on his account. This is so much more than a donation or some give-a-thon where you can text in a charitable amount. Compassion is all-encompassing. That means it's not limited to tears and money and volunteerism because it is a way of life. Those who hurt are not interruptions in the journey but rather part of the pilgrimage. And climbing down in the ditch where they may be bleeding out is not a distraction but part of the mission.

Heartfelt compassion causes us to intersect with those who are helpless and hopeless. And when we see the hurting as part of the journey, we realize we need them as much as they could ever need us. We go down into the ditch where the hurting live because Jesus is in that ditch. And because we follow Him, our pilgrimage will never bypass the pain of this world but will engage it head-on. This is compassion, and this is where Christ leads us.

Kindness: How We Relate to Others

While the word compassion focuses more on feeling, the word kindness focuses on how we relate to others. Certainly there is some major overlap with these two words because compassion does lead us to action. Nevertheless, there is a difference in meaning and application.

One scholar put it this way: "Compassion goes out to the distressed and suffering, goodness or kindness to all whom we can benefit."[3] In other words, kindness has a much broader application referring to how we generally relate to those around us. While compassion has to do with climbing down in the ditch with those who are hurting, kindness has to do with our everyday demeanor.

It almost feels like it should even go without saying: those who follow Jesus should be the kindest human beings on Earth. After all, "God's kindness is intended to lead you to repentance" (Rom. 2:4). God is kind and patient in allowing us to realize our sinfulness and thus change our mind and ways. So we—those who bear the name of Jesus and call ourselves "Christians"—should be kind to all who cross our path. We should be kind in our relationships, kind in our interactions on social media, kind when we leave a tip after a meal, and kind when we talk about people we don't even know. Kindness should be a key ingredient in the recipe that makes up a godly reputation.

And our kindness should be an obvious, standout part of the wardrobe of grace. Do you know anyone who wears loud-colored shirts? I'm not talking about a little pop of color in their outfit but rather an entire garment in a certain color that seems to say, "Hello everyone, look over here!" Well, our kindness should be that obvious, it should be that apparent, it should be that gregarious—but without even a hint of pretentiousness. If kindness were a color, then I believe it would be road worker orange or maybe hot pink. In other words, kindness is an unmistakable and distinct part of our spiritual attire. No one should have to look hard to see it.

Humility: How We View Ourselves

If kindness is the loudest part of our wardrobe, then humility might be the subtlest and the most cherished. As Calvin writes, "No one will be kind and gentle but the man who, laying aside haughtiness, and high-mindedness, brings himself down to the exercise of modesty, claiming nothing for himself."[4] Paul wrote in Philippians 2:3, "Do nothing out of selfish ambition or conceit, but in humility consider others as more important than yourselves." First Peter 5:5 expresses another aspect of humility: "In the same way, you who are younger, be subject to the elders. All of you clothe yourselves with humility toward one another, because God resists the proud but gives grace to the humble."

Humility was certainly not thought of as a strong or virtuous characteristic in the Greco-Roman world. Or maybe another way of saying it is that there was no place for humility in paganism. One Greek scholar put it this way: "The virtue admired by pagans was domination, powerful self-assertion, assuming a position above other men; hence humility was despicable to the pagan mind, a poor, low mind could not assert itself and lord it over anybody."[5]

Reading those words about ancient Greco-Roman society makes us realize not much has changed. We live in a world where self-worship is the religion of the day. Where self-assertion through social media dominates more of our time than we are willing to admit. We all have become photojournalists, and our favorite subject to cover is self. The more we can assert self, the more dominant and famous we become. Yeah, I would say that our culture has some striking parallels to the thoroughly pagan Greco-Roman world.

True humility is a rare virtue in a culture of self-worship. The humble person doesn't think anyone else is beneath her. Like Paul, who saw himself as the chief of sinners, humble people are so astounded by God's grace that they could never look in the mirror and think too highly of themselves. Humble people know that Jesus is sufficient and that they are totally dependent on His love and grace. Hence, they know who they are before the audience of God. They know they were created not with more or less value than anyone else.

How does God respond to the truly humble? Simply put, with favor. This is essentially what Jesus was teaching His disciples in response to their debate over who was the greatest, "If anyone wants to be first, he must be last of all and servant of all" (Mark 9:35).

The humble person is sometimes hard to find after a dinner party because he has quietly slipped out to wash the dishes. She may be difficult to spot at church because the spotlight isn't her goal. He can often be found helping to load the team bus while everyone else is jockeying for the best seat. Or maybe she's taking out the trash, just because she noticed it was full.

Humble people often see what others miss because everyone else is too busy seeing only themselves. Humble people are willing to do undesirable tasks even at inconvenient times because they desire to serve. And they serve not as a means to an end but as an extension of who they are.

They may even do something like preach the gospel for thirty years covering ten thousand miles and never get paid a penny for it.

Gentleness: Our Attitude toward Others

Just as kindness is closely allied to compassion, so gentleness shares some overlap with humility. Eugene Peterson calls this quality and piece of our wardrobe a "quiet strength" (Col. 3:12 MSG), and it is often translated "meekness." Gentleness has to do with the inward disposition or the attitude we have toward others. Gentleness is that inward disposition that enables one to accept the unfortunate consequences of a broken world and respond appropriately. It is an attitude that serves as a governor to the whole being so that we are responding reasonably as opposed to overreacting. Unfortunately, in our modern time, gentleness has become almost synonymous with weakness. Someone who is gentle is often thought of as having no backbone, but nothing could be further from the truth.

> This word connotes a submissive and teachable spirit toward God that manifests itself in genuine humility and consideration toward others. It is regrettable that the English word *gentleness* has come to have the popular connotation of a wimpish weakness and nonassertive lack of vigor. As an expression of the fruit of the Spirit, gentleness is strength under control, power harnessed in loving service and respectful actions. One who is gentle in this sense will not attempt to push others

around or arrogantly impose one's own will
on subordinates or peers. But gentleness is
not incompatible with decisive action and
firm convictions. It was after all "gentle Jesus
meek and mild" who expelled the mercenar-
ies from the temple with a scourge because
of their obstinate defilement of his Father's
house.[6]

As with so many of these qualities, gentleness seems foreign in our culture. Gentle people have the moral fortitude
to ensure their actions are bathed in care and concern. They
operate based on what they should do, not what they could
do. They are ever willing to do the greatest good and take the
most peaceable path.

This inward disposition isn't determined by fear or any
sense of entitlement but rather by love and humility. We
become gentle as we imitate Christ, who perfectly demonstrated strength under control and harnessed His power in
loving service and respectful actions.

When I think of gentleness, I imagine a strong dad who
works with his hands every day. His hands are calloused,
and the occasional scar serves as a reminder of the difficult
manual labor he regularly performs. He is tough and even
a bit rough around the edges, yet when he clocks out and
comes home to the family he works so hard to provide for,
he is immediately greeted by his young children. In their
excitement they never slow down as they run toward him
in the doorway screaming, "Daddy's home!" Because he is
gentle, he falls backwards, becoming almost pillow-like as
his children crash into him. After he sets his lunch pail down
and kisses his wife, he plays a game on the den floor that
involves wrestling and a lot of imagination. It's a game that
they, and so many other kids, have made up over the years.

One night he's a monster, the next night he's a dragon, and his children run around screaming while he attacks them with tickles. One should never allow the callouses on his hands to mean anything more than they do, for his heart is gentle and his spirit is sweet.

If gentleness were a person, he would be a dad tough and strong, who is also the gentle giant his kids jump on and play-wrestle with. He could hold their hands without squeezing too tight, he could toss them in the air only to catch them softly, and they could lay their heads on his chest and fall asleep while he put them in their beds, never interrupting their rest. Gentleness is a quiet strength.

Patience: Our Temperament toward Others

The patient pilgrim doesn't harbor feelings of resentment and revenge. He doesn't see or feel the need to react every time someone has wronged him. Nor does he hold a grudge because he keeps a mental register of all the times he has been treated unfairly.

Often the Greek word for "patient" is translated long-suffering. The word Paul uses here expresses patience under the ill treatment of others.[7] This piece of clothing is so important because it deters us from retaliation against those who have treated us unjustly. And, like the rest of the wardrobe of grace, this is countercultural because we live in a world where two wrongs seem to make a right.

The basis for our patience, of course, begins with God. We are taught in 2 Peter 3:15 to "regard the patience of our Lord as salvation." Through God's patience we found ourselves at the feet of Jesus; every Christian is redeemed because of God's patience. And as such we should be patient through and through.

The relevance of this word for our time cannot be over-stated. We live in a culture that will look, with increasing intensity, disparagingly on Christians. The list is ever grow-ing concerning ideas, values, and beliefs that Christians hold that are considered outdated and intolerant. Our culture believes it has evolved in views concerning sexuality, the family, bioethics and sanctity of life issues, medical ethics, and the list goes on. The point is that as Christians we hold to our beliefs without being bullheaded. We are to esteem what Scripture values without being viscous in our viewpoints. Jesus hasn't called us to fight for Him, as if He somehow needed us, but rather to be patient with those who would belittle or look down on our faith. The reason we have been given patience as part of the wardrobe of grace is because we will desperately need it. At some point ill treatment is inevi-table; patience, therefore, is invaluable.

Endurance: Our Perseverance with One Another

People aren't always going to act the way we think they should act. In fact, members of our own communities, small groups, and/or churches will offend us, whether intention-ally or unintentionally. The question then becomes, How do we respond?

Unfortunately, many are answering this question wrongly. If they don't like something in their church or community of believers, they leave or gossip or hold grudges. It's a take-my-ball-and-go-home attitude in response to others who have offended us.

The problem with this approach is twofold. First, responding to sinful behavior with more sinful behavior in no way brings about health or resolution. Second, the church community isn't bound together by tribal or individual pref-erences but by the gospel; we are trophies of grace that have all met at the foot of the cross. Therefore, if God's goodness has brought us together, how dare we let our preferences or even differences drive us apart?

Paul is basically saying, "Hey, even if someone bothers you or offends you, endure!" *Enduring* is putting up, tolerating, and forbearing with others even when they fail or act differently from what is expected.[8] In essence, members of a community are not to quit the community. Whether tempted by forces outside, such as persecution, or forces within, like gossip, quitting is never an option. The community of believers that make up the local church are not a club one can join and then discontinue at leisure. Community is all about doing life and experiencing Jesus together.

Bonhoeffer put it this way: "Where the body of Christ is, there Christ truly is. Christ is in the church-community, as the church-community is in Christ (1 Cor. 1:30, 3:16; 2 Cor. 6:16; Col. 2:17, 3:11). 'to be in Christ' is synonymous with 'to be in the church-community.'"[9]

In other words, we don't have the option of being "in Christ" and not being in the church. Rather, we are to endure, "bearing with one another" or as the New Living Translation puts it "mak[ing] allowance for each other's faults" (Col. 3:13). The culture at large should realize, as they see us, that the community of people who follow Jesus are not perfect, but they are bound together by perfect love. And because we are bound together by perfect love, we will persevere with one another as we journey onward.

We need to demonstrate that we are not the type of people who take their ball and go home, but rather we persevere because when all is said and done, followers of Jesus are together just trying to make our way home.

Forgiveness: Extending Grace toward Others

This is the only piece of the wardrobe accompanied with specific instructions: "Forgiving one another if anyone has a grievance against another. Just as the Lord has forgiven you, so you are also to forgive" (Col. 3:13). Paul is telling us that Jesus is our model for forgiveness.

So, how does Jesus forgive? Three words: *immediately, completely, eternally*. When I think of forgiveness, I imagine the prodigal son, who prematurely took his inheritance from his father, ran off to some foreign land, and wasted all the money. After he had partied like it was 1999 and all the money was gone, so were his so-called friends. A short time later he found himself homeless and starving, and in the midst of his despair, he devised a plan. *I'll go home, ask forgiveness,* he thought to himself, *and ask for a job as one of the hired hands.* With this reasonable plan firmly planted in his thinking, the son started the long walk home:

> "But while the son was still a long way off, his father saw him and was filled with compassion. He ran, threw his arms around his neck, and kissed him. The son said to him, 'Father, I have sinned against heaven and in your sight. I'm no longer worthy to be called your son.'
>
> "But the father told his servants, 'Quick! Bring out the best robe and put it on him; put a ring on his finger and sandals on his feet. Then bring the fattened calf and slaughter it, and let's celebrate with a feast, because this son of mine was dead and is alive again; he was lost and is found!' So they began to celebrate." (Luke 15:20–24)

What a beautiful picture of forgiveness! The father must have been waiting for his son to have seen him when he was still a long way off. Furthermore, the father didn't wait to hear the son's prepared speech about how he had sinned and didn't deserve anything. The more I read this text the more I think the son could hardly get the words out through the hurricane of celebration as he was being embraced by his father. His father, with tears in his eyes, kept hugging and kissing his son; meanwhile, the son is trying to say, "Hold on, Dad, I need to ask your forgiveness." But the father knew the son was sorry before the words were spoken. It's a great reminder that our Father God is more concerned with the condition of our hearts than any eloquent words we could express. And just like the father with the son that came home, our Father, through the redemptive work of the Son of God, fully restores us as His sons and daughters.

Yes, God forgives immediately and completely, but He also forgives eternally. Psalm 103:12 articulates this better than any other place in the Bible: "As far as the east is from the west, so far has he removed our transgressions from us." When God forgives, He forgives fully and forever. I don't need to worry about whether God will at some point in this pilgrimage bring my transgressions up and throw them in my face. God isn't going to remind us of how many times He has already forgiven us, as He reluctantly forgives one more time. When we sin and ask forgiveness, God never rolls His eyes and says, "Here we go again." No, He keeps extending forgiveness to us because, for those in Christ, He has already removed our sin from us.

And so Paul is saying, "The way God has forgiven you and the way God continues to forgive you, that's how you are to forgive others." I love the way The Message reads here: "Forgive as quickly and completely as the Master forgave you" (Col. 3:13). We are clothed in grace; therefore extending grace to others forever makes sense. That means the moment someone wrongs you and you have a complaint against them, you ought to extend grace and forgive.

How much healthier would our lives and relationships be if we consistently buried every complaint, every wrong ever done to us, in forgiveness? What if extending grace was simply a natural part of the rhythm of our lives? Especially since both the previous virtue—persevering—and this virtue—forgiving—are written in such a way as to communicate the habitual manner in which we are to exercise these qualities.[10] Let's just say that if these aspects of the wardrobe of grace were really articles of clothing, perseverance and forgiveness would be made from the most durable material.

Love: The Virtue that Makes All Others Possible

Love is the crown of the wardrobe of grace; it is the glue that enables the expression of the seven virtues and holds the community together.

The phrase "the perfect bond of unity" (Col. 3:14) is sometimes translated "the bond of completeness," and this is really the idea. Real love is real completeness. While the community itself isn't perfect, the love that completes the Christian and binds together the Christian community is. This goes back to Paul's central theme for the letter: Jesus is enough. Christ's *agape* kind of love completes the community. How could we ever improve on that? When God's kind of love becomes our focus, the community becomes unbreakable and the church unstoppable.

The term used for "love" is *agape*, the most common word used in the New Testament to describe God's kind of love. Four primary words communicate some aspect of our word *love* in the Greek language. The first two have to do with friendship, parenting or family, and the third describes the type of love reserved for the marriage bed. But *agape*, the fourth word, means to care for someone motivated by the love God has demonstrated toward us.

Agape is God's kind of love. So we love because God has loved us. We demonstrate love in the same manner that Christ has demonstrated love toward us.

Love is the virtue or quality that makes all others possible. The wardrobe is not just complete with *agape* but more accurately is put together with God's kind of love. It may well be that by clothing ourselves in the love of Jesus we also put on heartfelt compassion, kindness, humility, gentleness, patience, endurance, and forgiveness. In other words, God's love doesn't just complete the wardrobe; it determines it. And for a guy that has a hard time remembering all the different steps to tying a tie, the benefit of focusing on love is a blessing that cannot be overstated. In the end it all comes down to love. When love is the priority, then we present ourselves in a manner pleasing to the Lord.

Live like you've been chosen, like you are holy and cherished by God, like you are loved. And when we live knowing we are loved, our intentionality regarding all other attire— the full wardrobe of grace—becomes a natural expression of this sacred reality.

Six O'clock
From Tolerance to Togetherness

The all-too-familiar stench of men rotting away in pris-
ons and dungeons seemed to linger a little heavier approaching the six o'clock hour. So many thoughts, so many events
and ideas, so many years rushing through his mind like orga-
nized chaos. Paul saw himself as a pilgrim making his way to
a heavenly homeland, and he was now closer than ever. He
remembered the Damascus road and how Jesus stopped him
in his tracks, the glorious weight of purpose that had rested
on his shoulders all these years, the beauty of friendship, a
heavenly mind-set, and, of course, being clothed in grace.
What appeared on the stage in his mind's eye?

Could it be that in the six o'clock hour Paul pondered
the undeniable force that Christianity had become? That this
faith, this movement, which was begun by a renegade rabbi
from a remote region who turned out to be the Messiah,
was now an unstoppable influence on the world? That all
the house churches planted, the missionary journeys completed, the pastors trained, the people converted, the letters
written—that all of it revolved around one person who was
the one true God and one church made up of His people?

Christianity had become a litany of stories and communities that together attested to one irrefutable truth: Jesus is the Messiah; He is "the Lamb of God, who takes away the sin of the world!" (John 1:29).

Thinking such thoughts during the six o'clock hour, Paul must have been struck by the singularity of this movement. It had one cause and one mission, one aim and one chief objective, and he had been a part of it. He must have thought back on his desire that the church would be one, united under the banner of redemption, bound together by the experienced grace of Jesus. If Paul's pilgrimage could be summed up in a short amount of time, it would be: *He was a torchbearer for the gospel in a dark world, and once people's eyes were opened to the redemptive work of God in Christ, he prepared them to live a life worthy of the gospel of Christ.*

Paul had worked, not to build many churches but rather one church. The expression of this one universal church was local bodies of believers, also called churches, galvanized around the gospel of Jesus Christ. Paul dedicated his life to one overarching culture that certainly encompassed a multiplicity of subcultures. To put it in modern-day terms, Paul was a one-brand kind of guy: he preached Christ and Christ crucified.

My son loves football, and I mean he really loves it. He loves to play, watch, read, and talk about it. At present he plays football in an organization called Pop Warner. Pop Warner is the largest youth football league in the world. They have more than 300,000 kids playing football or cheering it on every weekend. I've always had great respect for their emphasis on safety and scholarship. In other words, they are teaching kids the basic fundamentals of football, and if you don't make good grades, you don't play in the game. Now Pop Warner teams play all over the country and even in several other countries around the world. Each individual team has a name like the Lightning or the Panthers, but each team is part of the large, overarching organization called Pop Warner. When trying to understand that Paul was part of one church, think of it in terms of Pop Warner. Throughout Paul's life he started a lot of churches like Pop Warner has a lot of different teams, but they were all part of one church, like how every team is part of Pop Warner.

That is, of course, not to say that churches should view themselves in competition with one another, as in the game of football. Rather we should live and be encouraged with the understanding that all the individual churches around the world are part of something bigger than themselves.

This is evident in how Paul addresses churches he planted or helped:

- "To all who are in Rome, loved by God, called as saints" (Rom. 1:7).
- "To the church of God at Corinth, to those sanctified in Christ Jesus, called as saints, with all those in every place who call on the name of Jesus Christ our Lord—both their Lord and ours" (1 Cor. 1:2).
- "To the church of God at Corinth, with all the saints who are throughout Achaia" (2 Cor. 1:1).
- "To the churches of Galatia" (Gal. 1:2).

We could go on and on, but the point is already becoming clear. There were local bodies of believers called churches, and each one of them was a part of the universal church, which refers to redeemed individuals everywhere, throughout time. Paul was keenly aware and convinced that the church could not be limited to one culture or ethnicity, one nation or geography. The gospel Paul preached was not and would not be contained by borders of any kind. And while the church would be full of churches with people who spoke in different languages, ate different food, wore different clothes, etc., from one locale to another, Paul believed they had more in common than not.

It's an amazing thought, isn't it? Take two cultures that at first glance have nothing in common with each other, cover them in the redemptive blood of Jesus, and they are now one people. While culture may describe us by pointing out that which differentiates, the redemptive work of Christ distinguishes us as one people.

Tolerance or Togetherness?

The gospel doesn't just cause strangers to respect one another. This, however, is the best the world can hope for. Unbelievers encourage us to respect those who are different, to live and let live, to tolerate the "other." But is tolerance really a high enough bar? Would you really feel loved if someone examined you and then said, "I guess I'll tolerate you"?

No, you wouldn't. And the good news is, the gospel calls us to a much higher standard. We are not merely to tolerate one another; the gospel takes strangers and makes them family.

I am always blown away by this reality as I travel. Whether in the Middle East, Asia, or Africa, when I meet a fellow Christian, more times than not I hear the following words, "Welcome, my brother!" People I have never met before refer to me, and I to them, using familial language. Why? Because in Christ we are all sons and daughters of God, part of the family of God, and therefore brothers and sisters in Christ. In one sense we are all journeying our way home to the heaven country for a family reunion. Fellow pilgrims are family.

Everything about the church seems to have the miraculous as a key ingredient. Jesus the Christ, the Messiah, redeeming a people, that movement forming into the church, that church being expressed in local churches all over the world, and those local churches made up of redeemed individuals brought into the family of God. The church of Jesus Christ isn't powerful because of tolerance; it is an unstoppable force because of its togetherness. And what makes togetherness so powerful? The tie that binds: redemption. The message is the gospel, and the mission is God's desired will, not the individual's. Probably no text demonstrates this better, or more succinctly, than Philippians 1:27–28:

> Just one thing: As citizens of heaven, live your life worthy of the gospel of Christ. Then, whether I come and see you or am absent, I will hear about you that you are standing firm in one spirit, in one accord, contending together for the faith of the gospel, not being frightened in any way by your opponents. This is a sign of destruction for them, but of your deliverance—and this is from God.

We live in a world of tolerance. Because much of our culture is largely comfortable with morality being something like Play-Doh that can be shaped into whatever image a mind can imagine, tolerance has become the prevailing sentiment of the day. To be intolerant of one's views, on morality in particular, has become like a cultural unpardonable sin. It's OK, according to these standards, to disagree, as long as you make statements like, "That lifestyle may work for you, but for me . . ." or "I believe you have the right to choose, but for me I have chosen to . . ." But the minute you don't add those qualifying statements, be careful my friends, you may be labeled as intolerant.

How are we to think and feel about all of this? We know as Christians much of our morality is fixed and therefore does not have the flexibility of soft clay to be shaped. For us the Creator has already shaped for us a moral certitude on things like marriage and the family or the sanctity of human life. Thus, we are guided by our convictions to care deeply and compassionately about such issues as poverty, racism, sex slavery, abortion, pornography, and the orphan crisis in our world. David Platt summarized this well in his book *A Compassionate Call to Counter Culture* when he wrote:

> What if the main issue in our culture today is not poverty or sex trafficking, homosexuality, or abortion? What if the main issue is God? And what might happen if we made him our focus instead? In a world marked by sex slavery and sexual immorality, the abandonment of children and the murder of children, racism and persecution, the needs of the poor and the neglect of the widow, how would we act if we fixed our gaze on the holiness, love, goodness, truth, justice, authority, and mercy of God revealed in the gospel?[1]

Platt is right. The church—all the churches—is going to have an incredible and positive impact on this world when the focus is the gospel. Gospel-centeredness drives and motivates our engagement in cultural change. We should care deeply about the injustices of this world because we believe deeply in the good news of Jesus. My hope is that we will discover what Paul knew deep in his soul: God's people are strongest when they are together. I believe this text provides for us a strategy that will help us move from tolerance to togetherness.

A Picture of Togetherness

One Identity: Live like Citizens of Heaven

As pilgrims, we do not wander through this world like free-spirited people devoid of direction and purpose. Nothing could be further from an appropriate picture. We wander as citizens of heaven. When Paul writes, "Live your life worthy . . ." he used a verb that could literally be translated "conduct yourselves as citizens."[2] Now, to fully understand the reason Paul used this word, we need a quick snapshot into the recent history of Philippi. To accomplish this, we turn to the scholarship of Robin Griffith-Jones and his summary of the context Paul was writing in:

> Philippi was the first of all European cities to hear Paul's good news when he sailed westward across the northern Aegean in 48. Philippi was a Roman colony, re-founded by Octavian (Augustus) after his victory at the battle of Actium in 31 BC. Roman veterans had been settled in the city; its full citizens were citizens of Rome. We cannot know how many of Paul's converts were citizens themselves or shared in the civic pride of the veterans' children and grandchildren. The rest of the population—the indigenous noncitizens—looked in at the Roman establishments

from the outside. But everyone in the city knew that the veterans' descendants were proud citizens of a commonwealth that embraced not just their own city, but the whole known world.[3]

So basically the city was divided into two groups of people: the haves and the have-nots. The dividing line between those two groups was whether you were on the inside or outside regarding citizenship. Into this divisive environment Paul instructs that whether your granddaddy fought in the battle of Actium or not, if you follow Jesus, you are a citizen of heaven. To those who were indigenous to the city, who felt their heritage had been devalued and discarded by the big bad Roman Empire, Paul reminded them of their heritage and future that were valued beyond any empire throughout all of history. You may be on the outside of the Roman Empire, he was saying, but you are inside the kingdom of God. Only the redemptive work of Christ could solve this issue. Paul was essentially saying, "Whether you can trace your roots back ten generations, or you just fought your way into the neighborhood a few years ago, you have one identity."

Togetherness begins with understanding identity. We are all woven into the fabric of God's redemptive story and have thus been granted heavenly citizenship. So the challenge becomes to live your identity, to live worthy of the gospel, to live like a citizen of heaven.

One Spirit: Unity Begins with Attitude

The unity of the local church begins with the attitude that should characterize the church.[4] Now, let's be honest about something here. The most significant chance for disunity in our local churches comes from within. It is important that we are humbly aware of this in a Western context: *The greatest danger for division will always be among the saints.* Blame it on pride, individualism, or even the entrepreneurial spirit; we have to be humble and wise enough to realize the church's potential worst enemy is often the face staring back in the mirror. We know from reading the next chapter that disunity can be caused by selfish ambition, vanity, a lack of humility, looking down on others, and focusing on one's own interests (Phil. 2:3–4).[5] This is why Paul begins his recipe for unity and togetherness with "standing firm in one spirit" (Phil 1:27) which is to say, the right "attitude."

Now, if unity has a recipe, there are only two ingredients, and the first is attitude. So the question becomes, What does this unified spirit or attitude look like? First, Christians can have the right attitude because they have been redeemed by the work of Christ and are indwelled with the Holy Spirit. In short, God has given us the necessary resources to have a good attitude. Therefore, we must choose to have an unwavering focus on the gospel throughout any event, especially during times of plenty and comfort.

An unhealthy attitude will creep in when we cease to be consumed with the awesomeness of God and the goodness of the good news. An unhealthy attitude creeps in when we think we deserve more than someone else. It creeps in when our agenda becomes the most important. The wrong attitude always emerges when we have the wrong focus. From Paul's words to the saints in Philippi, we should hear a clear message: focus on Jesus and let that determine your attitude, your temperament, and your outlook, so that you can be united. If the right attitude is the result of a focus on the gospel, then it could be said that attitude provides a community with a shared understanding. In the end it is amazing how much in life and the journey comes down to attitude. And

106   MOMENTS 'TIL MIDNIGHT

it's amazing how things can go so wrong so quickly with the wrong attitude.

One Mind: Unity Is Solidified in the Will of the Believers

A steadfast attitude leads to a consolidation in gospel-centered thinking and activity among the community. The word that is translated *mind* can also be translated *soul*. The idea here is that we be united not just because of a right attitude but also because of a united heart or mind-set.

Have you ever heard the phrase "the will of the people"? Well, that is the idea with this word for *mind* or *soul*. Being of one mind has to do with a people who galvanize around one purpose. Paul's hope was that the will of the community of believers in Philippi would be united. While there is some overlap of meaning in the words *spirit* and *mind*, both words are used here to shed light on the intangible qualities of a pilgrim. These two words together appear elsewhere in Paul's writings, for example, in 1 Thessalonians 5:23: "Now may the God of peace himself sanctify you completely. And may your whole *spirit*, *soul*, and *body* be kept sound and blameless at the coming of our Lord Jesus Christ" (emphasis added).

Notice how the spirit and soul were uniquely different from the body? When Paul uses these two words, he is talking about all nonphysical stuff, all that can't be measured or seen through a microscope or on an X-ray.

In our everyday vernacular we use the phrase "heart and soul" to describe the same thing. For example, when two lovers are trying to express the full weight of their emotion for one another, they may say something like, "I love you with all my heart and soul!"

The great reformer John Calvin helps us understand these two words when he refers to "standing firm in one spirit, with one mind" as a "two-fold unity—spirit and soul. The first is, that we have like views; the *second* that we be united in heart . . . 'spirit' denotes understanding, while 'soul' denotes the will." Think of unity like a coin where one side is heads and the other is tails. On one side of the unity coin is "spirit" (attitude) and the other side is "mind" (soul or will).

With all that said, probably the healthiest picture of the church being of one spirit and one mind can be seen just days after Pentecost in Acts 2:44–47 and then again in 4:32:

> Now all the believers were together and held all things in common. They sold their possessions and property and distributed the proceeds to all, as anyone had need. Every day they devoted themselves to meeting together in the temple, and broke bread from house to house. They ate their food with joyful and sincere hearts, praising God and enjoying the favor of all the people. . . . Now the entire group of those who believed were of *one heart and mind*, and no one claimed that any of his possessions was his own, but instead they held everything in common. (emphasis added)

One Mission: Unity Is a Team Sport

The study notes in the HCSB Study Bible summarize this idea well: "Harmony, not individualism, achieves God's purposes."[6] The phrase "contending together for the faith" is undeniably a sports reference to teamwork. You've probably heard the common phrase, "teamwork makes the dream work!" Well, it could certainly apply here.

The Greek word translated "working" is where we get our English words *athletics* and *athlete*.[7] Therefore, the verbiage

Paul uses is meant to create a word picture of teams contending for a prize. As corny and cheesy as it may sound, folks,
we are Team Jesus all the way! And the church is to work
together, as one unit, in one accord, toward this goal: "for
the faith of the gospel" (Phil. 1:27).

Ours is a united effort in which we are striving to be
in concert with the teaching of the gospel. The phrase "the
faith" is synonymous with Christianity. Paul is saying we
must contend; we must strive toward a unified understanding of the gospel. The Irish biblical scholar J. A. Motyer put
it this way: "There is no agreement unless there is agreement
as to what constitutes the gospel . . . the unity of the church
is a unity in the doctrine and the experience of salvation."[8]

Let it be said here and now: our togetherness is substantive. The unity and togetherness being talked about here are
not one born of compromise but rather conviction. We are
unified around the gospel and will contend for it because the
proof of its validity is a dual threat. On the one hand, each
member of the team has experienced the gospel, and it is
thus undeniably true to them and worth contending for. On
the other hand, the veracity concerning the doctrine of salvation is not left to one person's experience, for the historical
evidence leaves us with only one option on the scoreboard
of what is true. The church is, in one sense, then, a group
of people who have been chosen for Team Jesus, and they
believe in His message and mission through and through.

Finally, the church is most effective when its togetherness
for the gospel is intact. With the wardrobe of grace as our
team jersey, and the Messiah Himself as our captain, ours is a
team supernaturally bound together. We are one in the mission, that being the chief objective of Team Jesus, because the
mission at some point collided with our lives, and we have
never been the same.

One Enemy: Who Will Not Cause Fear among the Saints

Again the Greek language paints for us a helpful picture when wrestling with the phrase "not being frightened in any way by your opponents" (Phil. 1:28). The word for *frightened* stirs up a picture of a timid or scared horse. Paul was saying we should be like the horse who is not startled in anything, who doesn't get scared by every little noise or commotion.[9]

Ladies and gentleman, whether you've been on the journey of following Jesus five minutes or fifty years, you know that Satan is real. It's not necessarily popular to reference him, but he is the adversary, the devil, who is the enemy of God, all the saints, and all that is good. It may seem that the Christian has many opponents, but really those opponents are all puppets whose strings are being played by the one ultimate opponent to God and His people. In short, he is the enemy, and he is behind all that opposes the plans of God. Make no mistake about it, he seeks to impede the advancement of the gospel whenever and however he can—which is why the notion of opponents to the gospel are mentioned in this context.

When the church isn't united, the advancement of the gospel suffers. The enemy would desire nothing more than the church to be divided because divided we fail and united we obey. Because we have a common enemy and a common warfare, our minds ought to be united together in holy agreement.[10]

God has never looked at a sunrise and thought to Himself, *You know, this is gonna be a tough day.* Or, *Man, I don't know how we're going to handle all that stands in the way of My desired will.* God has never been stressed or anxious; God has never worried or wondered how a day would end. In the same manner, we as followers of Jesus should stand united and undaunted by any opponent, unalarmed by any unforeseen circumstance. God has never been intimidated, and neither should anyone on Team Jesus.

One last word concerning those who are "your opponents." They were once us before our pilgrimage began. We were enemies of God. They are enemies of God. God won us over; He loves them and wants to win them over. Our goal should never be to treat opponents like they are the opposition but rather to see them as an opportunity to bear witness to God's goodness in Christ Jesus. Our hope should always be that "your opponents" would one day become friends and family.

One Outcome: Earthly Opposition Is Evidence of Heavenly Deliverance

Why should we not be frightened by opponents? Because their opposition to God and His saints "is a sign of destruction for them, but of your salvation—and this is from God" (Phil. 1:28). Paul is not delighting in the destruction of those who oppose the faith. What He is saying is that a gospel-centered and thus united church stands as an ever-present sign or evidence that God's way leads to salvation, while the opposing side leads to death and destruction. Togetherness should be clear evidence that any way other than the gospel cannot be tolerated within the church. So this unity the church experiences serves as a witness and an invitation. Our togetherness should appeal to those who oppose the faith as if to say, "We are Team Jesus, and you can be part of Team Jesus as well!"

This is not to say there won't be suffering or hardship. Let me say this as clearly as I can: suffering is part of the Christian life. Paul wrote in 2 Timothy 3:12, "In fact, all who want to live a godly life in Christ Jesus will be persecuted." No pilgrimage has ever occurred divorced from difficulty.

The road to heaven isn't an amusement park ride you just board and get off once the ride is over.

We journey through the wilderness of this broken world getting banged up and bruised along the way. Because the opposition is real, there will be suffering, but we are not alone. This is why Paul writes about the togetherness of the church, and in other places, the sufficiency of God's grace. If anything, we learn that the enemy in his attack bears witness to the authenticity of our faith . . . we learn from these instructions to take heart when we suffer, for when we are suffering we are becoming like Jesus.

Final Thoughts on Togetherness

Looking at togetherness from every angle causes us to acknowledge:

- One identity as citizens of heaven
- One spirit demonstrating that togetherness begins with the right attitude
- One mind signifying that the will of the people has galvanized around the gospel
- One mission to please God through gospel-centered unity
- One enemy who will not intimidate the church
- One outcome showing God's way for God's people is victorious

There is little doubt in my mind Paul would have thought about the church as the hours passed in the Roman dungeon. He refers to togetherness as "just one thing" (Phil. 1:27) when articulating his thoughts to believers in Philippi. Their togetherness was Paul's primary objective.

With the passing of time, many things change and so much doesn't. The struggle for ministries and churches to remain united as one body, steadfast in their demonstration of the togetherness for the gospel, is real and sometimes publicly evident. My hope is that in a world of tolerance, we would realize God delights in His people's togetherness. Just as children are not born orphans but rather part of a family, so the sons and daughters of God are born—or rather, born again—into and thus part of the family of God. Something powerful and special can happen when we realize we are one church, part of one unstoppable force that is the movement of Christianity. Steadfastly united, there is no limit to the amount of good the church can do in a broken world; disobediently divided we will only end up on the sidelines as a parade of injustices passes us by. Tolerance may be the path of least resistance, but togetherness affords the church the opportunity to stand in the arena of culture and be a catalyst for what God wants, desires, and hopes for His world.

Seven O'clock
The Spirit of Alice . . . and of Paul

In Lewis Carroll's classic work *Alice's Adventure in Wonderland*, Alice is instructed by the White Queen that one must practice thinking about the impossible, saying, "When I was your age, I always did it for half-an-hour a day. Why, sometimes I've believed as many as six impossible things before breakfast." Of course Carroll's work would be adapted to the big screen in Walt Disney's 1951 movie *Alice in Wonderland*. I have always been fascinated with the world Alice finds herself in. Wonderland was a place where animals and even doorknobs could talk. It was a place of adventure and magic and peculiar friends like the Cheshire cat. I guess what I liked most about it was the ability to imagine a world that did not exist and then go on an adventure in it. It's an ability that has been largely lost on our culture today—the spirit of Alice.

With God, All Things Are Possible

I have to say it is a different world from the one we live in! In our world, it seems to the casual observer, that most of our experiences happen through some kind of screen or device. Our imaginations seem to be limited to decorating a selfie with the latest app or just editing ourselves into the person we wish we could be. We have more apps and games at our fingertips than we could ever use. We no longer have to wait the grueling seven days until our show comes on again. Nobody's got time for that! Now we just binge episode after episode away until we can no longer keep our eyes open. Even when we visit places of historical or cultural significance, our first thought most often has to do with where we can take a pic, so we can share that pic. We seem to be more into sharing or reporting an experience than having an experience. We've largely lost the ability to stare at a piece of art and lose time or to stand in a place of historical significance and imagine all that may have taken place there. The view from atop the mountain has been principally lost on us because we are too busy trying to make ourselves part of the landscape.

We live in a world of such technological advancement and luxury and—don't get me wrong—it's amazing! Think about it. In 2006 these technologies hadn't even been invented yet: the iPhone, iPad, Kindle, 4G, Uber, Android, Spotify, Square, Instagram, Snapchat, WhatsApp, and Pinterest. And surely by the time some of you are reading this, even these will be outdated!

But as consumers and benefactors of this tsunami of technological advancement, are there any downsides? Now, I'm just a casual consumer who on a weekly basis is usually holding a microphone in front of some crowd somewhere in the country, and many times that audience is referred to as "this generation." With that in mind, many of us seem to have settled for a secondary or simulated experience, as opposed to a primary or real experience. We experience life and the world around us through technology.

What if we are missing something by never looking up from our phones? What if we have traded in imagination and dreaming for digital interaction and downloading? Maybe we have subconsciously cleared some shelf space in our brains to make room for more of what technology makes possible. And in the process we discarded the desire and creativity to think about the not-yet-imagined ways we can change the world. What if there is an ocean of big problems just waiting to be solved, just waiting for someone to exercise his creative energy and do what everyone else thought to be ridiculously impossible. Well, it would seem—just from this casual observer's perch, mind you—that instead of setting sail in the ocean of possibility aboard a ship named *Wonder*, we are content lying on the sand and taking a selfie.

The world needs people who believe God can use them to accomplish what so many believe to be impossible— people who see that ocean of problems and are willing to set sail and solve a few. The world needs people who get lost in their own heads considering the forgotten and overlooked and think creatively toward answers. It needs those who are willing to ask questions others won't even consider, pilgrims who believe their journey is purposed to intersect with, not run from, the Mount Everest-sized crises in our culture. The types of pilgrims that believe God plus them can make up a majority any day of the week don't need a movement or an organization behind them before they act. They are sojourn-ers who dare to think and take to heart Jesus' words, "With God all things are possible" (Matt. 19:26).

Paul's life continually bore witness to Christ's words and to the words he wrote in Philippians 4:13: "I am able to do all things through him who strengthens me." His journey was

so amazing in part because he seemed continually to overcome all odds. I mean, let's be honest, Paul should or could
have died so many times along those ten thousand miles and
thirty-ish years as a pilgrim wandering this world:

- There were multiple attempts and plots
  on his life (Acts 9:23, 29; 20:3; 21:30;
  23:10, 12; 25:3).
- He was stoned and left for dead (Acts
  14:19).
- He endured satanic attacks and pressure
  (1 Thess. 2:18).
- He was beaten and jailed at Philippi (Acts
  16:19–24).
- He suffered name calling and ridicule
  (Acts 17:16–18; 26:24).
- He was falsely accused (Acts 21:21, 28;
  24:5–9).
- On five occasions he was given thirty-
  nine lashes by the Jews (2 Cor. 11:24).
- He was beaten with rods three times by
  the Romans (2 Cor. 11:25).
- He survived numerous violent storms at
  sea (2 Cor. 11:25; Acts 27:14–20).
- He was bitten by a poisonous snake (Acts
  28:3–4).
- He was forsaken by friends and co-laborers
  (2 Tim. 4:10, 16).[1]

All that and, not to mention, he spent nearly six years
in jail! Any one of the above mentioned events could have
been enough to bring his journey to an end. In the end all
one can do is marvel at the hand of God on this man, this
pilgrim, this apostle who lived his purpose, accomplishing

what so many would have deemed impossible. But not for Paul because he was God's "chosen instrument to take my name to Gentiles, kings, and Israelites" (Acts 9:15). And as God's chosen instrument, experiencing Christ's sufficiency, he had learned to be content in every difficult season. Paul's journey demonstrates for modern-day pilgrims that we can endure the harshest of circumstances "through [Christ] who strengthens me" (Phil. 4:13). The pilgrim can have wounds and still worship, scars and still attest to God's goodness.

Let us pretend for a moment that it's seven o'clock. The last bit of daylight is dissipating into the night. The dungeon is beginning its nightly cooling process as the stones respond to the cool night air starting to set in. Paul reconfigures his body in a pointless attempt to get comfortable. The sound of his chains reverberates throughout the dungeon. And his thoughts change direction as they already had several times that day. Now he is thinking, pondering really, on how God used him to accomplish the seemingly impossible. Observing the full scope of the journey, he shook his head in jovial disbelief. He may have even chuckled when he thought, *Shipwrecked and snakebit all in the same day.* I have no doubt he would have thought back on the words of Joseph, "You planned evil against me; God planned it for good to bring about the present result—the survival of many people" (Gen. 50:20).

The question for us modern-day pilgrims should be, *How do we rediscover the spirit or belief that God can accomplish His desired will, even if it seems impossible, through His people?* What can we glean from Paul's pilgrimage that would cause us to look up from our screens, jump on a ship called *Wonder,* and sail out to the big blue filled with opportunity for the people of God to make a significant difference in a broken world? Yes, the world is pretty messed up right now. So, how can our journeys make it better? And not just a little more moral than it was five minutes ago, but rather, how can we engage in such a way that it puts a spotlight on God's mission and redemptive work in this world? To do this we need to discover, or rediscover, the spirit of Alice, the spirit of Paul.

Recapturing the Spirit of Alice and Paul

Unshakable Belief: Do I Believe God Can Use Me?

Paul demonstrates for us on multiple occasions his unshakable belief that God called him and would use him to accomplish His purposes:

> "But the Lord said to him, 'Go, for this man is my chosen instrument to take my name to Gentiles, kings, and Israelites.' . . . Immediately he began proclaiming Jesus in the synagogues: 'He is the Son of God'" (Acts 9:15, 20).

> "Paul, a servant of Christ Jesus, called as an apostle and set apart for the gospel of God. . . . We have received grace and apostleship to bring about the obedience of faith for the sake of his name among all the Gentiles" (Rom. 1:1, 5).

> "I was made a servant of this gospel by the gift of God's grace that was given to me by the working of his power" (Eph. 3:7).

Paul knew that he had been singled out, that God had called him to this amazing task. He believed in the depths of his soul that God could accomplish this task and accomplish it through him.

Paul was part of a growing list of characters in Scripture that God had chosen to demonstrate His sufficiency to accomplish His desired will for His creation. So we can probably assume that Paul was in good company with those who believed deeply that God could use them:

- Noah *had never* seen rain . . . much less an ocean.
- Sarah *had never* been pregnant.
- Joshua *had never* fought a battle or led a nation.
- David *had never* killed a giant.
- Josiah *had never* been king.
- Nehemiah *had never* built a wall.
- Esther *had never* been queen.
- Jeremiah *had never* rebuked a nation.
- Zechariah and Elizabeth *had never* been parents.
- Mary and Joseph *had never* been parents.
- Most of Jesus' disciples *had never* been chosen until that renegade rabbi from the back side of nowhere walked along the seashore of their lives.
- James *had never* believed, much less led a church in a major city.

And, of course, Paul had never led a movement. He had never planted a church or gone on a missionary journey. He certainly had never been imprisoned or beaten for his beliefs.

He could probably have filled pages with stuff he had never done.

God doesn't wait for our résumé to be just right before He decides to use us for a specific task. Many of us will probably never feel ready. If anything, most of us feel overwhelmed or underqualified at the thought of stepping out and doing something for God. We may certainly feel undeserving of any door of opportunity the Lord may open to us. But Paul teaches us that God can use the most unlikely candidates to accomplish some of the most amazing tasks. In each circumstance from the list above, grace gifts were given so that the formerly unimaginable became a reality in their obedience. In the tapestry of God's story, He repeatedly specializes in using those who "had never" so that in each circumstance redemption continues to be the theme and Jesus is forever the hero.

We could easily add (insert your name here) to the growing list of unlikely suspects God chooses once again to demonstrate His sufficiency. In every example used, the same feeling existed. This doesn't come down to feeling God can use you. Feelings are overrated. I'm talking about believing God can use you! And when you believe God can use you, you will discover that you are in good company, my friends, good company indeed!

Sacred Gifting: How Has God Gifted Me to Help Change the World?

Paul believed God in His infinite wisdom has given each person talents or gifts:

> For by the grace given to me, I tell everyone
> among you not to think of himself more
> highly than he should think. Instead, think

sensibly, as God has distributed a measure of faith to each one. Now as we have many parts in one body, and all the parts do not have the same function, in the same way we who are many are one body in Christ and individu- ally members of one another. According to the grace given to us, we have different gifts. (Rom. 12:3–6)

We have all been given different gifts, and these gifts are to be used to benefit and make the church function as it could and should. In 2 Timothy 1:6 he writes, "Therefore, I remind you to rekindle the gift of God that is in you through the laying on of my hands." Obviously Timothy's gift was pastoral ministry. But I believe the application of this text, certainly when also considering Romans 12:3–6, is that we have all been given gifts, and God expects us to use those gifts for His purposes.

Paul continues his explanation of our gifts:

If your gift is serving others, serve them well. If you are a teacher, teach well. If your gift is to encourage others, be encouraging. If it is giving, give generously. If God has given you leadership ability, take the responsibility seri- ously. And if you have a gift for showing kind- ness to others, do it gladly. (Rom. 12:7–8 NLT)

So the question becomes, How have you been gifted? What are you good at? Your gifting is no accident, so steward your abilities well. I used to have a friend who would say often, "You're not one in a million; you are one in a cre- ation." There is a lot of wisdom and truth in that statement. God didn't "break the mold" when He made you because

122 MOMENTS 'TIL MIDNIGHT

there was no mold. He made you infinitely unique and infinitely valuable.

Another way of looking at it is to say your uniqueness has value to God's purposes. So discover your gifts, fan the flame that is that gift, and let it shine. Steward the talents and gifts God has given you so they burn bright. Not to bring attention to self but rather to the One who gave the gift in the first place. Find out what you're good at, recognize that it came from God, and then use it to make Him obvious throughout the journey.

Enduring Vision: How Will I Use My Gifts to Accomplish Change in the World for the Glory of God?

Paul never lost sight of the original vision God wanted to be accomplished through his life:

> Nevertheless, I have written to remind you more boldly on some points because of the grace given me by God to be a minister of Christ Jesus to the Gentiles, serving as a priest of the gospel of God. My purpose is that the Gentiles may be an acceptable offering, sanctified by the Holy Spirit. Therefore I have reason to boast in Christ Jesus regarding what pertains to God. For I would not dare say anything except what Christ has accomplished through me by word and deed for the obedience of the Gentiles, by the power of miraculous signs and wonders, and by the power of God's Spirit. As a result, I have fully proclaimed the gospel of Christ from Jerusalem all the way around to Illyricum. My aim is to preach the gospel where Christ

has not been named, so that I will not
build on someone else's foundation. (Rom.
15:15–20)

Paul had a vision—something the world had never seen.
He believed in an idea that most in Jerusalem would have
deemed impossible. He believed it and held on to it years
before it would ever come to fruition. How did Paul want
to change the world? What was this vision? He believed a
Gentile could become a Christian without becoming a Jew
first.

Now I know what you're thinking: *That's it?! That's Paul's
dream, his vision, the thing that doesn't exist that he wants to see exist?!*
Yep! Let me explain.

There was a prevailing belief among many Jews that
in order to become a Christian, one must also adhere to
certain aspects of the Jewish religion. They were teaching
that "unless you are circumcised according to the custom
prescribed by Moses, you cannot be saved!" (Acts 15:1). In
the presence of Paul and Barnabas, some of the Pharisees
turned Christian emphasized this all the more, declaring of
the Gentiles, "It is necessary to circumcise them and to com-
mand them to keep the law of Moses" (Acts 15:5). Certainly
this is contrary to the message Paul was preaching. This leads
to the Jerusalem Council, which was basically a conference
made up of apostles and elders from the Jewish religion who
gathered to decide whether Gentile believers needed to be
circumcised and follow the Mosaic law. During this council
Peter gives the authoritative answer. Listening to his words,
one could easily have imagined them coming from Paul:
"On the contrary, we believe that we are saved through the
grace of the Lord Jesus in the same way they are" (Acts 15:11).
Peter affirmed sound theology based on the gospel, which

happened to be the vision that drove much of Paul's life: faith alone, grace alone, and nothing else is required.

Now remember the great task God gave Paul in Acts 9:15: "To take my name to Gentiles, kings, and Israelites." Also keep in mind that the word *Gentiles* refers to all non-Jews. Paul was a vessel to powerfully preach so the world would hear the gospel. While God's redemptive work has its roots in the nation of Israel, the mission of Christ is that the gospel will be heard and experienced among every language, tribe, ethnicity, and people group throughout the world and throughout the ages. Paul was certainly charting new territory.

I love movies, and in recent years I have become particularly fascinated with Pixar films. They are amazing in so many ways: the plot, humor for both kids and adults, the music, and of course, the incredible technology. I recently read the story of how Pixar came to be under the leadership of Ed Catmull. He currently serves as the president of Pixar Animation and Disney Animation.

Ed grew up in the fifties with his two childhood heroes being Albert Einstein and Walt Disney. Catmull recalls, "To me, even at a young age, they represented the two poles of creativity. Disney was all about inventing the new. He brought things into being—both artistically and technologically—that did not exist. Einstein, by contrast, was a master of explaining that which already was."[2]

Disney would have a more enduring impact on Ed, primarily because once a week *The Wonderful World of Disney* visited his family's living room via the television. As Ed Catmull was drawn more and more into the imagination of all things Disney, especially with movies like *Peter Pan* and *Lady and the Tramp*, he wanted to be an animator. The problem was that he had no clear pathway to become a Disney animator. So he shelved the idea and went off to school at the University of Utah.

Over the coming years he studied physics and computer science. He worked a short time for The Boeing Company and The New York Institute of Technology before returning to the University of Utah to work on his doctoral degree. Two things happened during this time in Catmull's life. First, he earned his PhD in computer science in 1974. And second, he began to recognize that art and technology could come together.

This idea evolved into a vision: he wanted to create the first computer-animated film. He believed this dream could be accomplished in ten years; unfortunately it would take twenty.

The idea of a computer-animated film was new territory; no one had ever done this before. Catmull recognized this: "Just as Walt Disney and the pioneers of hand-drawn animation had done decades before, those of us who sought to make pictures with computers were trying to create something new."[3] It would be a little while before Pixar, as we know it today, would come into existence. Ed was given the opportunity to direct the team of the Computer Graphics Lab back at The New York Institute of Technology. Here he would begin to put together a core team that would evolve into the nucleus of Pixar. From New York he landed his next job with none other than Lucasfilm, where he would serve as vice presedent of Industrial Light and Magic in the computer graphics division.

George Lucas was keenly interested in the role of computer graphics in movie making. Star Wars had just experienced worldwide success at the box office, and the crew was busy working on the follow-up The Empire Strikes Back. At this point the Pixar Image Computer was created over the course of about four years. This was "a highly specialized standalone computer that had the resolution and processing power to scan film, combine special-effects images with live-action footage, and then record the final result back onto the film."[4]

This is the first time we see the word Pixar appear in Catmull's journey. One of his colleagues wanted the name Radar, and the other wanted to use a made-up word Pixer. The result was a compromise, and the word Pixar was born.

In 1986 Steve Jobs saw potential in this division at Lucasfilm and decided he wanted to buy it. Catmull notes in his book that this was for the best because while George Lucas had worlds of ambition, he didn't share in Ed's dream to make a computer-animated film. While several notable companies were interested in buying Lucasfilm's digital division, Jobs would acquire it for five million dollars in 1986 and founded it as an independent company called Pixar.

The vision for Pixar's being a film-making company was probably not what Steve Jobs was buying. He had recently been basically fired from Apple, the company he started, and wanted to use Pixar in his future endeavors. For several years after Jobs purchased Pixar, it lost a lot of money. He personally invested fifty-four million dollars of his own money into the company and tried to sell it a few times. The problem was that Pixar Image Computers were too high end for the average company, much less the average household, to purchase. In the end Pixar sold only three hundred computers. Additionally, they created and sold software and made some commercials between 1986 and 1991.

Three things happened during this five-year period that helped Pixar eventually get on its trajectory of computer-animated films. First, they maintained a healthy relationship with Disney, who was certainly one of their most important customers. Second, they distinguished themselves at being creative and proficient in producing commercials. And third, John Lasseter won some awards for making computer-animated short films such as Tin Toy in 1988.

Over at Walt Disney Studios, there was a growing appetite for something new. Evidence for this was that The Nightmare before Christmas was in production and was planned for release in October 1993. So in 1991 Pixar entered into a contract for three computer-animated films with Disney—the first would be a movie called Toy Story. When Toy Story released on November 22, 1995, it was the highest grossing film on its opening weekend. It would later be nominated for three Academy Awards and was reviewed as one of the best-animated films of all time. The contract and overall business relationship between Disney and Pixar was renegotiated, and eventually Disney purchased Pixar in 2006.

I think it's safe to say that when Toy Story hit the big screen, history was made. The animation film industry that had produced such films as Snow White, Pinocchio, Bambi, Sleeping Beauty, Lady and the Tramp, and many more had been revolutionized. The genius of Walt Disney himself had been so long missed, and we, the audience, longed for genius to be reborn. Pixar satisfied that longing. Ed Catmull had a dream that turned into a vision for a computer-animated film. The success of Pixar is largely the success of a vision that refused to go away—a vision that endured.

Enduring vision is attractive. That someone else endured and believed for such a long time, that they were convinced in their minds and souls in the soundness of their ideas is both comforting and motivating. Paul had such an enduring vision. Shortly after his conversion on the Damascus road, he would preach his first sermon (Acts 9:20). The idea that Gentiles could become followers of Jesus and not have to go through the Jewish religion is an idea that would take time before it could take hold. Nevertheless, just as Pixar released one great computer-animated film after another, so Paul began to plant and spread the gospel to one city after another in the Greco-Roman world in which he lived. Paul was used to launch a movement that would become a worldwide force for good. What began on one road in Paul's life would be carried down every road, impacting millions of lives in the years to come.

Tenaciously Patient: Is My Patience Motivated by God's Grace toward Me?

Paul, throughout his life, sought to be tenaciously patient because Christ had demonstrated extraordinary patience toward him. Furthermore he would list patience as a virtue of the life that walks by the Spirit:

> But I received mercy for this reason, so that in me, the worst of them, Christ Jesus might demonstrate his extraordinary patience as an example to those who would believe in him for eternal life. (1 Tim. 1:16)

> But the fruit of the Spirit is love, joy, peace, patience, kindness, goodness, faithfulness, gentleness, and self-control. The law is not against such things. (Gal. 5:22–23)

Paul lived in a world where correspondence, travel, and work took a great deal of time. There were no shortcuts, systems, or software. If you wanted to get from one city to another, you put one foot in front of the other. Or you took your life in your own hands by sailing unpredictable seas. In any case, Paul's world required the steady and hard grind that is only displayed in a strong work ethic. And because the world turned a little slower two thousand years ago, it required a patience that is often not seen today. But I am convinced that with the right motivation it can be rediscovered.

Today's world is spinning at such a fast pace that it can almost make one dizzy. Yesterday I responded to emails from people all over the United States, texted about thirty different people, interacted with friends on social media from many different countries, had sushi for lunch and Italian for dinner—oh, and did a video conference call with a ministry in South Korea. And that was a pretty normal day! When my wife goes shopping, she will often FaceTime me to show me items before she buys them. If I'm on the road, I can watch my kids' games or recitals on my phone (just for the record, I try not to be gone during those important events). According to the experts, apparently knowledge is doubling every twelve months.[5] So when I say the world is spinning at a fast rate, you better take your motion sickness pills.

Paul moved slowly, but the progress of his ministry spread, at some point, like wildfire. We move faster, but spiritual progress seems to have died down to a slow crawl. The reasons for this are numerous, but the point is that there has never been more of a need for pilgrims to be tenaciously patient with our dreams, the vision, the journey, God's timing, and all the rest. The source for our patience is to focus on God's patience with us.

This is what Paul was essentially saying in 1 Timothy 1:16. His writings demonstrate: "God is endlessly patient with even the worst of sinners. Need proof? Just look at me!" God has not grown more impatient with sinners over the years like some old person who gets frustrated with any inkling of incompetence. First, God doesn't age. Second, just look at God's grace in your own life! I've never met a Christian who wasn't grateful for God's patience with him in coming to salvation. Remember, He is the father sitting on the front porch waiting for us prodigals to come home. And when we do, He runs to greet us. God is patient, and this should serve as endless motivation for the pilgrim to be tenaciously patient in the journey.

In rediscovering the spirit of Alice and of Paul, an easily overlooked quality is patience. Do you have a vision for how you want to use the talents God has given you? Are you wanting, even longing, for God to use you to do something significant, maybe something others would call impossible? "Dear friends, while you wait for these things, make every effort to be found without spot or blemish in his sight, at peace. Also, regard the patience of our Lord as salvation, just as our dear brother Paul has written" (2 Pet. 3:14–15).

Unwavering Focus: Am I Representing the Name of Jesus in Whatever I Do?

Paul wrote in such a way that it not only demonstrated focus in his life but also how all pilgrims could live a life of focus:

> But always pursue what is good for one another and for all. Rejoice always, pray constantly, give thanks in everything; for this is God's will for you in Christ Jesus. Don't stifle the Spirit. Don't despise prophecies, but test all things. Hold on to what is good. Stay away from every kind of evil. (1 Thess. 5:15–22)

> So, whether you eat or drink, or whatever you do, do everything for the glory of God. (1 Cor. 10:31)

Paul had a laser-like focus when it came to the purpose of his life. Whether it was a meal or a missionary journey, packing for a trip or planting a church, listening to the waves hit the boat or writing a letter to the saints, Paul demonstrated focus.

If we are to recapture this spirit—the belief that in Christ all things are possible—then focus is important. The key to focus or avoiding distractions will not be found in creating endless boundaries and parameters. Things like fasting from your phone one hour a day, limiting your social media usage, or how much you will watch television. These ideas and hundreds of others like them are all good, and I'm sure well intentioned, but eventually we create a life of rules and guardrails that resemble child rearing more than mature faith.

Paul teaches us that the key to avoiding distractions is to stay focused on living for the Lord. Distractions come when we divorce certain activities from our identity in Christ. To stay focused means that I keep everything in perspective, that the activities of my life marinate in my identity in Christ. Focus is thus a by-product of intentionality. So if I want to live a life of unwavering focus, I must desire for the entirety of my life to be done for God's glory.

Collaborative Friendship: Who Are My Friends That Will Help Me Change the World?

While most of Paul's friends abandoned him for various reasons at the end of his life, it is safe to surmise that he enjoyed a cohort of co-laborers for the gospel throughout his ministry. Such companions included:

- *Barnabas* (Acts 4:36–37; 9:27; 11:19–24; 11:27–30; 13:1–14; 15:1–2, 12)

- Silas (Acts 15:22, 27, 32, 40; 16:19, 25; 18:5)
- Priscilla and Aquila (Acts 18:2, 18, 26; Rom. 16:3; 1 Cor. 16:19; 2 Tim. 4:19)
- Luke (Acts 16:10; Col. 4:14; 2 Tim. 4:11; Philem. 24)
- John Mark (Acts 12:25; 13:5; Col. 4:10; Philem. 24; 2 Tim. 4:11)
- Timothy (Paul's traveling companion and the recipient of 1 and 2 Timothy; he additionally appears in the greeting in six of Paul's letters: 2 Corinthians; Philippians; Colossians; 1 and 2 Thessalonians; and Philemon.)
- Titus (Gal. 2:1–3; 2 Cor. 7:5–16; 2 Cor. 8:16–17, 22–23; Paul addresses one letter to him bearing Titus's name.)

While an entire chapter has already been written on the topic of friendship, at this point there is only one aspect to be added to the subject. All of Paul's co-laborers were just that: men who tirelessly labored with him to further the great task God had put on his life. These men were not buddies who came alongside Paul because of common interests. They didn't share hobbies; they weren't in a fantasy football league together giving each other a hard time on a weekly basis depending on how their players performed. Nope! They had one purpose and one purpose only: to labor with Paul in advancing the faith into new territory. They wanted to see scores of Gentiles believing in Jesus and growing in the faith. All of Paul's friendships revolved around the mission.

Every pilgrim needs a group of friends that are different from the typical friends drawn together by common interests. This is a cohort of co-laborers not bound by preferences but compelled by a common purpose. These are friends or co-laborers who serve one another with one goal in mind: to accomplish the purpose of God for your life. These types of friends can rarely be derailed into discussions about the temporal or trivial. It's not that these friends aren't fun to be around; it's just that we need some co-laborers in our life who feel time is short and the mission is too important to leave unaccomplished. There is a sense of urgency about them, just as there is a sense of urgency about you. These friends could be understood as a band of brothers or sisters, who are going to journey well and share with you the sacred weight of purpose because they are a cohort of co-laborers dedicated to the cause of Christ.

Christ's Strength: Do I Rely on the Extraordinary and Relentless Power of Christ?

Paul had an obvious emphasis on the sufficiency of Christ and relying on His strength in all situations:

> I am able to do all things through him who strengthens me. (Phil. 4:13)

> But he said to me, "My grace is sufficient for you, for my power is perfected in weakness." Therefore, I will most gladly boast all the more about my weaknesses, so that Christ's power may reside in me. (2 Cor. 12:9)

> I pray that he may grant you, according to the riches of his glory, to be strengthened with power in your inner being through his Spirit. (Eph. 3:16)

The nature of Paul's journey required that he rely on Christ's strength as sufficient for him to endure and run the race well. And while most of us aren't on boats in unpredictable weather, spending night after night in jail, or suffering the physical pain of being tortured because of our faith, we still have a desperate need to rely on Christ's strength. We need Christ's strength to remain focused, to remain pure, to remain courageous, and the list could go on. The more broken our world becomes, the greater the need to rely on the strength of Christ to stay faithful in it. The spirit of Alice and of Paul is all about believing that God "is able to do above and beyond all that we ask or think according to the power that works in us—to him be glory in the church and in Christ Jesus to all generations, forever and ever. Amen" (Eph. 3:20–21). Those who have rediscovered the spirit of Alice and Paul have simultaneously begun to understand the reliability of Christ's strength.

A New Breed of Thinkers

The world needs a new breed of thinkers—people who are ever aware of God's grace in their lives and thus believe that with Christ all things are possible. Those who dare to dream something new and accomplish something others would deem ridiculously unfeasible. The world needs people enthralled with possibility, driven by an optimistic realism rarely seen in the average bystander. People who see themselves as pilgrims prepared to journey into the heart of hell on their way to heaven. Pilgrims who believe their one journey can impact the world.

In one of my other books, I wrote about the subject of imagination and how to use it to creatively solve the problems of this world. At one point I issued a challenge that I originally wrote on an all-night flight at 2:00 in the morning. I now feel it would be a fitting end to this chapter which has focused on rediscovering the spirit of Alice, the spirit of Paul.

Here is to the dreamers of the day

those redeemed renegades who dare to
look out a different window

those who refuse to believe the present
situation is "as good as it gets"

go on, dreamers of the day, with your conscious dreams

your imaginary thoughts about real things

go on and imagine how it could and should be

go on in the name of God under the
banner of his redemption

find solutions where others only found problems

help the hopeless with an enduring conviction
that the redeemed are not helpless

open doors that have been closed and
kept shut by closed minds

rebuild walls when many have grown
comfortable with the routine of rubble

ask the questions no one is willing to ask

seek the answers that have been long
lost due to stalled imaginations

be fully human in a world that
increasingly devalues human life

turn a thought into a revolution and a
wild hair into a wonderful life

go on, dreamers of the day, as if the sun were
setting and your time is now or never

pick up your million-to-one ideas
realizing God never played the odds

let your visions and ideas find their infinite possibilities
in a reflection of the one who is infinitely creative

refuse the comfort of conformity and pathetic
outcome of pessimistic thinking

carry the torch of your idea if you be the only one

your flash of genius will not go unnoticed

unleash your courageous ponderings as if someone's
life depended upon their actualization

take action, initiate, as if your life depended upon it

become intoxicated by your redemptive imagination

may you only find rest when you slip away to slumber

may the imaginations in the day only be
interrupted by the dreams of the night

militantly refuse to compromise while at
the same time branded by the compassionate
nature of your imagination

oh dreamers of the day, carry on until it is carried out

catch a fire and set the problem ablaze
with your redemptive imagination

not because you can . . . but because you must

because grace demands more and never less

because the redeemed never take a time out

because the mission of God leaves you no other option

choose this because you have been chosen

motivated not by problem or even the solution first

but rather be supremely motivated by the
position granted you by the grace of God

go on, dreamers of the day, with
your redemptive imaginations

because you live at the feet of Jesus.[6]

Eight O'clock
The Art of Conversation

The darkness is settling into the cooling dungeon and with it a weight that is almost tangible. The hour is growing closer.

I wonder if Paul looked up from the oversized pit and could see the faint flicker of a torch being lit for the guards above. Down below such luxuries were rarely granted. The stones were now cool, and the night probably offered a sense of calm for Paul, who had a certain amount of experience being incarcerated.

I can't help but wonder if at this hour Paul thought to himself that the absence of light meant no more opportunity for correspondence. Something as simple as the light of the day or brightness from a torch made it possible for him to communicate so much through the written word. Maybe darkness was a trigger to think fondly on all the doors of opportunity God had granted him to converse about Jesus, the church, and righteous living.

In total Paul wrote thirteen New Testament letters under the inspiration of the Holy Spirit. These letters demonstrate Paul's brilliance as a teacher, his ability to articulate and eloquently persuade all kinds of people, and to do all for the cause of Christ. In short, he was a master communicator with both the written and spoken word. At this point Paul may have reflected on the vast number of people, churches, and cities God had allowed him to connect with, as is clearly demonstrated when glancing at the landscape of his correspondence.

1. When he wrote to the Romans, he was at the height of his mental ability. This letter was Paul's expressed desire to impart spiritual strength to the believers in Rome. The content distinctly articulates essential Christianity and those things that are matters of indifference. If Paul's writings were an art gallery, Romans would be the ceilings of the Sistine Chapel.

2. In 1 Corinthians Paul uses the full arsenal of stylistic devices to show that all believers belong to the Lord. He used more than seventy-five idioms, everything from irony to alliteration to hyperbole, all in an attempt to persuade his readers to accept the Lord's authority over their lives.

3. Second Corinthians is the letter that gives a backstage pass to the heart of the apostle Paul. The central theme is the nature of true ministry as he offers a strong and positive defense for his own authority and ministry.

4. In Galatians, Paul sounds the alarm and rings the bell of freedom in Christ. His

most intense letter, Galatians gives a declarative presentation of "the truth that sinners are justified and live godly lives by trusting in Jesus alone."

5. In Ephesians we are offered "an anthem to the sovereign grace of God displayed towards sinners in Christ."[1] The gospel is clearly the good news, as Paul demonstrates: "you were dead in your trespasses and sins. . . . But God . . . made us alive with Christ" (Eph. 2:1, 4–5). Therefore, because of this grace we are to "walk worthy" (Col. 1:10) according to God's good news.

6. Philippians is "Paul's most warmly personal letter"[2] because he is writing to say thank you for a gift the Philippian believers sent him while he was imprisoned. Paul wants them to be unified in their faith and to follow the example set by Jesus to be humble and live in service to others.

7. Colossians is written to correct heresy and false teaching that had found its way into the church. This letter presents a clear picture "of Jesus Christ as supreme Lord of the universe, head of the church, and the only One through whom forgiveness is possible."[3]

8. First Thessalonians is intended to address some questions the newly planted church and young believers were asking. Paul wrote in a fatherly tone to assure believers

in Thessalonica of the return of Jesus so they would therefore not lose joy or hope.

9. In 2 Thessalonians Paul is exhorting believers to stand firm in the faith in the midst of growing persecution. Continuing some of the exhortations from the first letter, Paul writes about how to live useful lives in light of the reality of the return of Christ.

10. In 1 Timothy Paul is writing to his younger co-laborer regarding living out his faith and shepherding others to do the same. The essence of Paul's first letter to Timothy could be summed up: "Don't let anyone despise your youth, but set an example to the believers in speech, in conduct, in love, in faith, and in purity. Until I come, give your attention to public reading, exhortation, and teaching" (1 Tim. 4:12–13).

11. Paul's final letter, written from the Mamertine Prison in Rome, was to Timothy, the young man he had discipled and been a spiritual father to for so many years. Second Timothy reads as final words, a kind of last testament, encouraging Timothy to remain faithful in his calling even in the midst of growing hostility toward the church and its leaders.

12. Written in a similar tone and time frame as the letters to Timothy, Titus is likewise encouraged to continue in the good work

and reminded that leaders in the church should be blameless in character, devoted to preaching, and should have the ability to defend and teach sound doctrine.

13. Philemon is Paul's shortest correspondence and the only letter of a private nature. In it Paul is writing as a friend to his friend Philemon about Onesimus, a runaway slave who had stolen from his master. Paul's desire in sending Onesimus back to Philemon with this letter was that the master would accept Onesimus back not as a slave but as a Christian brother.[4]

"Longhand Conversation" Defined

The notion of "longhand conversation" is an idea that has been, for the most part, lost in our day and age. This kind of communication bids its listeners to consider beyond surface level thoughts and engage at a level that could be called critical thinking. When one can articulate something important well, it summons the recipient of such content to wonder things they have never wondered before. It causes them to see a fresh perspective on an oft-familiar subject, or it may help them start asking the right kind of questions. In this way communication is a two-way street, whether it is a table of people engaged in conversation over a meal or an audience designed to be on the receiving end of content.

I've spent the better part of my adult life preaching and teaching to audiences, mostly made up of teenagers. And even though I am communicating to them as I preach or teach the Scriptures, I am aiming for much more than downloading content into the inbox that is their brain. I am attempting to engage the room, whether it's ten or a thousand, with images through storytelling, explaining historical context, and ideas that help them live fruitful lives as people of faith. I want to help them think differently than they may have previously, to be a guide in framing the right questions, and to point them to the right answer. I want something about the way they think or live to change as a result of our time together in God's Word. In this way I view communication through the lens of a conversation.

We communicate in a wide range of ways throughout our pilgrimage. An attempt to even list out the ways we communicate to an array of different audiences would be a monumental task to say the least. I hope we can glean from Paul, in his eight o'clock hour, the transferable principles concerning the art of longhand conversation that we can apply no matter the relationship or the audience. But first, a word of caution.

Entertaining Ourselves to Death

We live in a day when critical thinking has gone on a permanent sabbatical. And it makes sense. When a society becomes consumed with consuming, our consumerism elbows out such things as the ability, or even the desire, to think deeply, to ask penetrating questions, to think critically, and thus to communicate with one another. In our digital world of streaming and binge watching, we are losing something valuable. We are entertaining ourselves to death, and we don't even know it.

In a world where we don't think, we don't really communicate. At least, not in meaningful ways. We post stories for our followers to watch, we update our social media platforms, and we share our likes or dissatisfaction in sound bites and reviews. Sure, we lend our voice to the value of a product or show by reviewing and rating it, but that's not a conversation; it's just an opinion.

And therein lies much of the problem. Because we live in a society of one-sided conversation, our communication has become diluted. The ability to converse has been replaced with the willingness to comment.

But at the end of the day, if we have any desire to experience true community—the kind where people share life together and hurt with one another and celebrate with one another, the kind that's not limited to just showing up to a building once a week to hear some good preaching and sing a song or two—then we need to recapture the ability to interact through meaningful communication. After all, community can't happen when we limit our interaction such that our vehicle engine is still warm when we get back in the car to go home.

A Semi-disclaimer

A real conversation is a two-way street. You've been around those people who just talk because they like to hear themselves talk. When you sit with them and try to converse, the feeling of futility arises as they pontificate. You feel as if you are just a prop, someone to take up space on the other side of the table so they feel validated. You are there so they don't appear to be having a conversation with themselves, even though that's what is actually happening. In this scenario you are nothing more than window dressing.

The purpose of this chapter is: this is not that. While listening is an art and also an ability that has been largely lost on us, this chapter is about having something to say. And figuring out how to say it well.

If Paul was a Jedi knight at communication, then we are all Padawan learners. He could arguably dive deeper into truths and ideas than any other person in human history. He was like those pearl divers who dive 150 feet without the aid of tanks and then bring up a treasure. They have mastered the ability by conditioning their lungs so they can hold their breath longer than what seems humanly possible. Paul was the king of pearl diving—he could hold his breath, dive deep, and come up with treasure to share with the rest of us. We all need to make ourselves learners from this master of communication.

Pauline Principles

Now we turn our attention to learning something about communication from the Jedi master. Granted, the principles of communication I have extracted from Paul's writings are concise to say the least. Entire books themselves could be written dissecting the intricacies and idiosyncrasies of his correspondence. What I attempt here is to outline the principles that will aid in recapturing the lost art of longhand conversation. In other words, *What principles will aid me in thinking and formulating ideas that engage? How do we communicate in such a way that we are not just demonstrating critical thinking, but our communication is a catalyst for others to do the same?*

This is the aim, but let us keep in mind this was never Paul's ultimate goal. We have already delineated his purpose and his dream and, of course, seeing it all through the lens of Paul the pilgrim seeking to wander well in a broken world. But while instructing the principles of communication wasn't Paul's goal, we would be foolish not to take serious note of it.

A Warm Greeting Is Never a Wasted Word

We noted earlier that Paul began every letter praying grace and peace over his readers. There is something to be said for the warm greeting Paul always employed, even when he was dealing with sensitive issues. For example, in Philemon, Paul had to deal with a potentially sensitive issue. Paul's end goal was that his friend would be obedient in dealing with Onesimus upon his return. This is expressed in verse 21 when he writes, "Since I am confident of your obedience, I am writing to you, knowing that you will do even more than I say."

The letter is only twenty-five verses long, but one never gets a sense of conflict or even confrontation, though Paul desires for his friend to set a disgraced slave free and treat him like a brother. That tone of accentuating the positive is demonstrated right out of the gate as he writes, "To Philemon our dear friend and coworker, to Apphia our sister, to Archippus our fellow solider, and to the church that meets in your home. Grace to you and peace from God our Father and the Lord Jesus Christ. I always thank my God when I mention you in my prayers" (Philem. 1–4). On and on Paul goes, building up in an effort to bring about change. There is a lesson to be learned for how believers should communicate with one another when discussing sensitive and potentially conflicting points of views: *We are more likely to change others' views when we edify and expect them to do what is best and what is right.*

You've probably heard the old phrase, "You catch more flies with honey than you do with vinegar." An essential element in the art of longhand conversation is genuine kindness. One can never go wrong building up with words. The kindness we express will, more times than not, be the gateway to getting others to open their ears and having a receptive spirit.

Let me be as clear as I possibly can be: the way you begin any conversation, no matter the medium, will drastically influence the effectiveness of the message that follows.

Make Sure Your Content Supports Your Central Idea

Paul always had an agenda, a central idea at the heart of his message. Paul was always trying to make an undeniable point, and he used a wide variety of methods to make it. A. T. Robertson was a New Testament scholar who taught in the early 1900s; he pointed out how Paul clearly did this in one of his lectures:

> The heart of his argument turns on the fact that Jesus made propitiatory offering for our sins by His blood on the cross, which offering is mediated to us by faith in Christ as our Redeemer so that God freely justifies us and declares us righteous and will ultimately make us righteous. There are great words in Romans like righteousness, sanctification, redemption, propitiation, faith, justification, power, reconciliation, salvation, no condemnation, life, victory, sons, adoption, heirs. But they are all meaningless to Paul, apart from Christ. Christ is here seen as the sole means of righteousness, the sole hope of redemption, the pledge of all good. In Christ we are more than conquerors.[5]

We can learn something here about the art of longhand conversation—a sacred simplicity in having one idea around which all others revolve. And that idea, if it is truly formulated in our minds, should fit in one sentence or statement. Any communication with multiple theses is like a box of puppies turned loose, running in every direction. In other words, without a central idea that is continually supported, we will have no clear pathway in our thought, and ultimately we will not reach our goal.

This is particularly hard in a world where a million messages are floating around us at any given time. A friend of mine used to say, "We have the focus of an AM radio station on scan." Nevertheless, if the dialogue in the pilgrim's journey is going to be meaningful, it needs to be intentional. Intentionality requires a central idea that you want to communicate throughout the multiplicity of mediums we engage. And to have a central idea we must identify that central idea. For Paul in Romans it was the work of Christ in the believer's life. But let's break this down and make it practical.

I am particularly close to a handful of guys in my life. I would bare my soul to these men, and they would bare their souls to me. When I have the rare treat to sit down with one of them for a few hours, eat some good food, and have some laughs, I want to know how they are personally doing. My central idea, my agenda, is their well-being. A friend used to say it to me this way: "Brent, how's your soul?" I've never forgotten that little question, and I carry it with me into these types of conversations. I love my friends, and I want to know if their souls are good. Throughout our time we may chat about family, work, hobbies, sports, or any number of things; but all of that revolves around and supports the main thing.

Look Your Audience Square in the Eyes, Even if You Aren't Standing in Front of Them

At this point we get to the component of longhand conversation that involves the not-so-fun task of correction. The church at Corinth had a real problem. The immorality that characterized the city had found its way into the congregation. Henrietta Mears, in her bestselling book, *What the Bible Is All About*, wrote of the church in Corinth:

> The wonderful church at Corinth, the brilliant jewel in the crown of Paul's labor, was failing. It was all because the worldliness (carnality) of the city had gotten within its walls. It was all right for the church to be in Corinth, but it was fatal when Corinth got into the church. It is a glorious sight to see a ship launched into the sea, but it is a tragic sight when the sea gets into the ship. The church of Christ should be set as a light in a dark place, but woe unto the church when the wickedness of the world invades.[6]

When Christians begin to live like Jesus is not the central reality in their life, the health of the church will undergo sharp decay. To put it another way, when we forget the grace of Jesus, our stories always take a sad and tragic turn. Yet, in the midst of this, Paul didn't lose his temper and fill the letter with angry statements. But neither did he avoid confronting the issues of worldliness in the church. He was pastoral in his approach. He was firm and affectionate, providing clarity on his expectations without being harsh. And yet Paul was fiercely concerned with the purity of the church. Therefore, he was not afraid to make the tough decision regarding a person sleeping with his father's wife being removed from the congregation in hopes that the man would ultimately be restored.

The sheer volume of variety in Paul's language—he uses more than seventy-five idioms—demonstrates a profound sense of intentionality. Because Paul was having to correct the church in Corinth, he may have spent more time crafting this letter than any other.

We can learn so much from how Paul confronted the immorality in Corinth. First, he may have been absent in the body, but he spoke directly to them: "I'm not writing this to shame you, but to warn you as my dear children. . . . For I became your father in Christ Jesus through the gospel" (1 Cor. 4:14–15). Second, he spends a great deal of time accentuating the positive of what could and should be and less time speaking about specific sins. The logic here is that the good news of Jesus becomes overwhelmingly clear to the point that when gross immorality is mentioned it feels foreign and thus has no place in the church. Finally, there is a strong message of hope concerning the future when he writes: "Death has been swallowed up in victory. Where, death, is your victory? Where, death, is your sting? The sting of death is sin, and the power of sin is the law. But thanks be to God, who gives us the victory through our Lord Jesus Christ!" (1 Cor. 15:54–57). Paul, the master communicator, confronts with kindness, accentuates the positive of what could and should be, and provides hope for today and for the future.

Know How to Speak the Language of the Audience without Compromising Your Own Voice

Paul was a man capable and willing to wear many hats in an effort to fulfill the purpose of evangelism throughout his pilgrimage. When it was time to debate, he could debate with the best of them; when it was time to teach or preach, he could do so with any audience. He was comfortable communicating with royalty or high-ranking military and could just as easily interact with people in the marketplace from different parts of the Roman Empire. Probably no text demonstrates this better than 1 Corinthians 9:19–23:

> Although I am free from all and not anyone's slave, I have made myself a slave to everyone, in order to win more people. To the Jews I became like a Jew, to win Jews; to those under the law, like one under the law— though I myself am not under the law—to win those under the law. To those who are without the law, like one without the law— though I am not without God's law but under the law of Christ—to win those without the law. To the weak I became weak, in order to win the weak. I have become all things to all people, so that I may by every possible means save some. Now I do all this because of the gospel, so that I may share in the blessings.

This ability to become "all things to all people," this aptitude to speak the language of the audience in front of him, demonstrates something profound concerning Paul's character. A thread of selflessness was intrinsically woven throughout his pilgrimage. He had a closet full of hats because he was a servant of God and thus a servant of people. What we should take away from his skills to communicate to people all over the spectrum is that at the core of his being was a desire for people to know God. This servant's heart, this humble spirit, bled through his conversations. In the end he tried "to please everyone in everything, not seeking my own benefit, but the benefit of many, so that they may be saved" (1 Cor. 10:33).

Communicate the Profoundly Complex with a Sacred Simplicity

History is not short on intelligent people. History is short, however, on intelligent people who are capable of communicating complex ideas with a simplicity the average person could understand. Paul had the incredible ability to put the cookies on the lower shelf for the rest of us to enjoy.

I read and reread some authors, getting something new each time. I see something I didn't before, or I gain a deeper understanding or appreciation for a concept. There is something rare and powerful when someone can make the grandest and most mysterious of ideas attainable and achievable for the rest of us.

Think about this for a moment: with the exception of 1 and 2 Timothy, Titus, and Philemon, the rest of Paul's letters were meant to be read aloud to churches made up of everyone from children to educated adults. Paul writes, most of the time, with a particular congregation or network of congregations in mind. Therefore, he writes for the "everyman" in that church or churches.

In American history Thomas Jefferson, one of the founding fathers, possessed this rare quality. Pulitzer Prize-winning author Joseph J. Ellis explains that John Adams, another founding father, played a key role ensuring that Jefferson would be the principle author of the Declaration of Independence:

> Adams knew Jefferson could summarize complicated arguments quickly and gracefully, as he had in his 1774 "Summary View of the Rights of British America" and the 1775 declaration on the "Causes and Necessity of Taking Up Arms." Jefferson's aim in the declaration was not to break new philosophical ground, but to prepare a platform on which everyone in Congress, and in the states represented, could stand. It had to be clear, not

controversial, and utterly consistent with the country's prevailing mood.[7]

The ability to summarize something complicated for the common man—*"We hold these truths to be self-evident: that all men are created equal; that they are endowed by their Creator with certain unalienable rights; that among these are life, liberty, and the pursuit of happiness."* I would say Mr. Adams's assessment of Mr. Jefferson was spot-on.

And so it is with Paul, and so it should be with all who desire to engage the art of longhand conversation. Some subjects, ideas, philosophies, and doctrines will fascinate you and gain an enormous amount of your attention. You will, for all practical purposes, be an expert in those subjects. But as you grow in your knowledge, also grow in your ability to explain what you know in a manner others can understand.

Albert Einstein was known for saying, "If you can't explain it simply, then you don't understand it well enough." I think all would agree that Paul could explain the gospel simply. He knew it well enough.

The Smaller the Audience the Greater the Significance

The Bible contains only three individual letters from Paul to three people: Timothy, Titus, and Philemon. Still we have multiple conversations between Paul and small audiences in Scripture as well: consider Lydia's conversion in Acts 16:11–15, the jailer-warden in Acts 16:25–34. Of all the small audiences Paul addressed, 2 Timothy is probably the one that stands out the most to me. When someone knows he is sharing his last words, those words are calculated and profound. Furthermore, the recipient of those last words demonstrates who was a priority to them, even in their dying moments. Timothy's development as a leader and pastor, as a co-laborer and son . . . these things were a priority in the mind and heart of Paul.

I have a friend that teaches effective communication, and he is fond of saying, "The smaller the room, the bigger the stakes." And it's true, isn't it? When the conversation is intimate, everything is amplified, and the decisions somehow seem weightier.

One of my favorite examples of this in history is John Wesley's last letter. John Wesley led a movement of revival in England and North America, along with his friend George Whitefield, that significantly altered the immoral trajectory of the country. He was famous for saying, "The world is my parish," which is to say that he felt God had called him to a worldwide mission. He traveled four thousand miles annually and preached nearly forty thousand sermons in his lifetime.

One of the causes Wesley was involved with was opposing slavery and the slave trade. While he objected to slavery in writing, petition, and speech, all of his labors were in vain. Three days prior to his death, he rolled out of bed and slowly walked across the hall to his study. He sat down and penned his last letter. It was addressed to a young man in Parliament named William Wilberforce, who had just announced his intense opposition to the slave trade. Though the two had never met, the letter was profoundly valuable to Wilberforce. Here is a portion of that letter:

> Unless the divine power has raised you up to be as "Athanasius against the world," I see not how you can go through your glorious enterprise in opposing that execrable villainy, which is the scandal of religion, of England, and of human nature. Unless God has raised you up for this very thing, you will be worn out by the opposition of men and devils. But

if God be for you, who can be against you?
Are all of them stronger than God? O be not
weary of well-doing! Go on, in the name of
God and in the power of His might, till even
American slavery (the vilest that ever saw the
sun) shall vanish away before it.

Though Wesley's audience was small, being just
Wilberforce himself, the decision of opposing slavery would
be an increasing weight, and the encouragement to move
forward was amplified. And so it is with any communication
of this kind—the decisions seem weightier, and the content
seems amplified. Because the smaller the audience, chances
are, the bigger the significance.

Let Your Communication Contribute to Illumination

We should communicate in such a way that no matter
the subject, we are illuminating our audience. Whether your
audience is one person over a cup of coffee, a boardroom
of coworkers, a social media platform, or an auditorium
full of attendees, when you communicate, it should be like
someone just turned on the lights. By this I do not mean that
everything that comes out of your mouth or through your
keyboard should be an explicit gospel presentation. I am saying that the art of longhand conversation enlightens listeners
and recipients.

How do you know when someone has been enlightened?
They may ask more questions, but that could just be curios-
ity. They may say things like, "I'm going to think on that
some more," but that could just be a compliment. When
people have been enlightened, your communication has led
to illumination and then to application. In other words, our
communication should be a catalyst for some kind of change.

If people don't do anything with what we have said, then we have to ask ourselves, "Was it worth saying?" People always vote on your effectiveness in longhand conversation with the way they live their lives.

> My hope is that we will seek to recapture the art of longhand conversation.
>
> My aspiration is that we will take note from Paul, the Jedi knight of communicators.
>
> My desire is that we will glean and learn all we can about his approach.
>
> My longing is that we will illuminate others in such a way that they would change their minds and hearts . . . and thus change the way they live as children of God.

Nine O'clock
Grace Demands More

The Many Adventures of Nannie-Sue White

You can't put a price tag on a life well lived. I've met only a handful of people in my time who have truly lived well and died happy with God. One such person was born many years ago on the heels of the worst economic depression our country had ever experienced. It was a rough time that called for people to be thick-skinned and to apply a cold logic in their approach to life. It was not a season in this culture of countless options and the luxury of being picky. You worked where you could find work, and you survived hoping and looking to a better future for your children.

During this time two people who seemingly had little in common found each other and decided to get married. The husband wasn't a kind man and continually struggled with his inner demons. His immediate family, for reasons that are not completely known, had disowned him some years earlier. The wife was nearly twenty years his junior and seemed to be a person full of faith, life, and optimism. She wrote poetry about the sufficiency of Christ during hard times and taught

her children the Bible. This rather odd couple just so happened to be my great-grandparents. And what happens next is
still hard for me to understand, much less put down on paper.

Following their marriage, they did what most couples do:
they started having children. At that time it was common to
have many children in an effort to create more stability and
resources for the home. My grandmother happened to be
lucky number seven out of nine children. She recalled to me
a few years ago sitting in her north Georgia mountain home
the following.

One evening when she was a little girl, she was playing at a friend's house and having a great time making mud
pies. The sun was setting, her cue to begin walking home for
dinner. As she approached their dirt driveway, she was met
by some neighbors who informed her, along with the other
siblings, that their mother was inside the house giving birth
to their new sister. The scene inside the house was far from
joyful. In truth, her mother and the baby had died in child-
birth, and they were waiting on an ambulance to come and
remove the body.

I don't really blame the neighbors for the misguided way
they attempted to help. I mean, it would be a heck of a thing
to have to tell children that their mother was now dead.

Imagine the new situation: you have a single dad, who
is probably in his fifties, with eight children for whom he
was now solely responsible. His decisions that followed were
his decisions alone, and I refuse to judge him for them, but
I firmly believe, like the rest of us, he would ultimately have
to answer to God for the course of action he took. He started
sending the kids away to live with different relatives. I don't
know how he decided to send each child, but I can tell you
my grandmother got the bad end of the deal. At the age of
nine, her father placed her, along with one other sister, in an

orphanage. This is long before the foster-care system we have today or group homes, as they have come to be called. During this period of history, orphanages weren't always regulated, and many times they struggled with overcrowding. And so the orphanage is where my grandmother made her home from age nine throughout much of her teenage years.

The only reason she didn't age out of the system at eighteen was because an older sister who had gotten married came back and rescued the two sisters. I worked up the courage to ask her once about those years spent in the orphanage. She replied in a steady voice, "It was a bad time, and bad things happened, but God is good, and we don't need to talk about it." She would go to her grave never speaking of the years in the orphanage.

But her story would soon take another redemptive turn when one night she agreed to a sort of blind double date. The only problem was the gentleman she was matched with didn't exactly catch her eye; but her friend's date seemed like someone she would like to know. The two would eventually get the chance to go on a date together, and shortly thereafter they fell in love.

They decided to get married in Ohio, which was a considerable distance from the handful of relatives with whom my grandmother had maintained a relationship. This led to another scene that is hard to imagine. In July 1946, in a little church, my nineteen-year-old grandmother found herself standing in a beautiful white dress and no one to walk her down the aisle. In fact, because of the considerable distance and lack of funds, she had no family or friends present to witness the celebration. Assessing the situation—remember she is sharing this story with me at the age of eighty-seven—this nineteen-year-old bride-to-be grabbed the train of her dress and knelt alone before God in the back of that church. She expressed to Him that it was a good day, a day when God was making things new, a day for beginnings and not regret because it was a day a new story would be told. With that she stood to her feet and with flowers in hand awaited the music that would be her cue.

In July 1946 she did begin a new story. She walked down that aisle alone but walked out of that church hand in hand with a man that would love her unconditionally all the days of his life. She may have walked into that little church with a broken past and an uncertain heritage, but she walked out already feeling at home and feeling hopeful about the future.

The orphaned child was now Mrs. Sue White, married to a wonderful man named Gene. His work took them to New York where they lived in a quaint little apartment for a short time and then back to Ohio, living in Cincinnati and Cleveland, where they would have all four of their children, including my mother.

Eventually they resettled in Atlanta, Georgia. During their marriage they helped plant a church in Cincinnati, and then in Atlanta they helped as faithful members serving in a variety of roles. She took a particular interest in serving what was referred to as "juvenile delinquents" through a ministry in their church. Really they were just kids who had made some bad mistakes and needed someone to care for them. She also served throughout her entire adult life in a ministry focusing on refugees who had escaped Laos during the war-torn years in the 1970s. Her husband was involved in everything from serving as a deacon to singing in the choir to being church treasurer. Theirs was a wonderful marriage spent raising their kids, loving Jesus, and serving in their local church.

I was the first grandchild that came along and at an early age gave Sue White the unfortunate nickname of Nannie. Following the death of my granddad, whom we called Pop, she focused much of her time being around her children and grandchildren.

I grew up knowing my grandmother well, and in my adult years our phone conversations would last well over an hour. She was an avid reader, and when the Kindle and Nook came out, she devoured as many as 150 books a year. I mention that only to say this: hers was a life well lived, a story well told. She lived a life of excellence in all the arenas of her life: work, church, family, culture. All of it.

For me the exclamation point on this well-lived life came on Christmas Eve 2014 when I had the opportunity to baptize one of my children. I'll never forget my little girl taking my hand and walking down the steps into the water. Once she was positioned, I began to address our church. As soon as I looked out from the baptistery pool my eyes went to a fragile eighty-eight-year-old lady sitting in a wheelchair parked in the front of the auditorium. She sat there with tears in her eyes and a look of overwhelming joy on her face as her firstborn grandson baptized her great-granddaughter. She would live only a few more years until going home to the heaven country.

Hers was a life well lived, a journey worth remembering because the narrative of her life had redemption as its theme and the Redeemer as the central character. The many adventures of Nannie-Sue White demonstrate to us that a life of excellence is one that continually reaches for the highest good. A life of intentionality, service, goals, and accomplishments demonstrates all the fruit that springs forth from being rightly motivated. The life that is motivated by the work of Christ in us seeks to live well in response. The phrase "grace demands more" may sound counterintuitive or even harsh, but if you have experienced the grace of God, then you know it bids you to live a life of a different standard, a life that seeks the highest good in all things.

Pauline Excellence along with a Word from His Good Friend Peter

It is nine o'clock. This was certainly not the first nine o'clock hour Paul had spent in the darkness of a prison or dungeon. But this time it was different because this time would be the last.

With each passing moment he was growing more aware of the imminent and swift conclusion rapidly approaching his existence on Earth. So many amazing thoughts and ideas had already danced across the stage in his mind's eye, each providing him with a measure of comfort and encouragement. He had journeyed for so long and so far, and he had achieved so much in his time. I wonder if in these moments, chained down in the darkness, he reflected on all God had allowed him to be a part of. I wonder if he ever took a deep breath, exhaled, and said, "Whew! What a journey it has been." Maybe he felt a sense of calm and comfort as he considered not a perfect life but one that sought to please God, a life of excellence.

Ted Engstrom was an amazing evangelical leader whom God used in so many ways—including helping Billy Graham launch his crusades, leading Youth for Christ, and revitalizing World Vision. In the early eighties he wrote a short book called The Pursuit of Excellence. In it he describes how Paul was a man of excellence:

> Paul was a man of particular brilliance, trained at the feet of the great Gamaliel in the traditions of ancient Israel. Through study and experience, he learned to be comfortable in both the world of the Greek and the Jew. He was an orator of no small merit and a man who would compose some of the most

NINE O'CLOCK: GRACE DEMANDS MORE

poignant letters—from some of the surprising places—ever recorded in the history of
humanity. This man of such great academic
and spiritual accomplishment could have
rested on his laurels. He could have lived as
if he had arrived, but he didn't. He put aside
the past, lived in the present, and pressed on
toward the goal of conforming himself to the
image of his Lord."[1]

Paul saw himself as in process, having never arrived. And
this served as motivation to pursue excellence in all things.
This is probably why the subject of excellence appears on
more than one occasion in Paul's writings.

And I pray this: that your love will keep on
growing in knowledge and every kind of
discernment, so that you may approve the
things that are superior [excellent] and may be
pure and blameless in the day of Christ. (Phil.
1:9–10, emphasis added)

And now, dear brothers and sisters, one final
thing. Fix your thoughts on what is true, and
honorable, and right, and pure, and lovely,
and admirable. Think about things that are
excellent and worthy of praise. (Phil. 4:8 NLT,
emphasis added)

Whatever you do, do it from the heart, as
something done for the Lord and not for
people. (Col. 3:23)

> Be diligent to present yourself to God as one
> approved, a worker who doesn't need to be
> ashamed, correctly teaching the word of
> truth. (2 Tim. 2:15)

Mr. Engstrom is correct that excellence ought to be a standard we seek throughout our pilgrimage. And while we can achieve it, we are never to rest in that achievement. Therefore, it is continually sought. One of my favorite texts pertaining to excellence is found in 2 Peter 1:3–4 (ESV):

> His divine power has granted to us all things
> that pertain to life and godliness, through the
> knowledge of him who called us to his own
> glory and *excellence*, by which he has granted
> to us his precious and very great promises, so
> that through them you may become partak-
> ers of the divine nature, having escaped from
> the corruption that is in the world because of
> sinful desire. (emphasis added)

When we are made new in Christ, God has "granted to us all things that pertain to life and godliness." We have been given everything we need to live a life that is pleasing to God, a life of excellence. In fact, He has called us to a life of virtue and excellence that we "may proclaim the excellencies of him who called you out of darkness into his marvelous light" (1 Pet. 2:9 ESV). God has shared with us everything we need to live a life that, in turn, motivates us to praise and put a big spotlight back on God's redemptive work. This is the notion of excellence to which Paul and Peter are referring. This was the life my grandmother lived, and this is the kind of life that all who journey are called to live.

Excellence Defined

Paul and Peter are clear that we are called to a life of excellence. But what does this look like? Practically, how do we pursue excellence? There are several keys to keep in mind.

Excellence is a standard rooted in our understanding of God. Excellence can't be reduced to a mere goal within the journey; rather, it is a standard for the journey. That standard begins with God. Those of us journeying homeward shouldn't ascribe to excellence because it is a good idea in the larger scope of culture or because business leaders with accolades a mile long have written on the subject. Rather, this standard has been determined because of our view of God and how He has revealed Himself to us in Scripture.

We matter so much to God that He paid off our massive sin debt, which we could never do in a thousand lifetimes, with the blood of His Son. He has purchased us from the death we surely deserved. This was the understanding of grace Paul had, and this understanding should lead all of us to believe: *grace demands more, never less.* A right view of grace should bid me to lay the entirety of my life as an offering at Jesus' feet. In short, grace experienced calls me to a life of excellence.

New Testament scholar Andreas Köstenberger supports this idea: "God is a God of excellence, and if you are a Christian, he has called you to pursue excellence in everything you do, whether in the personal, moral, or vocational arena."[2] God's work in our lives is our starting point for framing this idea of excellence. Köstenberger wrote a book on this subject titled *Excellence*. The following quotation has been essential in shaping my definition of excellence:

> Excellence is particularly important when the
> pressures of sheer survival and mediocrity

are particularly intense. The primary reason for this is bound up with the nature and character of God. God is the grounds of all true excellence. He is the one who fills any definition of excellence with meaning, and He is the reason why we cannot be content with lackluster mediocrity, half-hearted effort, or substandard scholarship. Without God as our starting point our discussion of excellence would be hopelessly inadequate.[3]

Excellence is a decision and an achievement. With God as our starting point, we must turn our attention to personal responsibility. Excellence is about becoming or making the decision to continually aim at a standard that is pleasing to God. This does not contradict the reality that, in Christ, God is already pleased with us. We don't aim to earn His favor; we aim to please and glorify Him because He has already shown us favor.

The highest good should always be the goal in the journey. We are to seek the highest good throughout the various dimensions of our lives—home, culture, vocation, church—because we seek to live a life that makes Jesus proud.

If you buy into this approach concerning excellence, you will begin to notice some changes—changes like a low tolerance for mediocrity in your journey. Being average becomes something other people do but not you. Excellence achieved gives you an appetite you never even knew you could have. It's like when you start to eat healthy and discover you actually enjoy it. Then after months of food that's good *and* good for you, the idea of a fast-food diet is a notion you just can't stomach! Excellence achieved, and continually achieved, is like maintaining a right diet that in and of itself is the highest good.

But just because you have a new appetite, a new standard that is being achieved, doesn't mean you look down on others who pull through the drive-through of mediocrity every day. You don't despise it for others; you just loathe the notion of settling for less in your own life. After all, you only have one journey, one pilgrimage, just one chance to wander this world. So, why not wander well?

Alas, excellence is an achievement, or rather a series of achievements. Again, we are not approved by God because of our achievements, but we seek to achieve excellence because God has already approved of us. Throughout history, because some people were born into a certain family or at a certain time, they had opportunity thrust upon them. They may have inherited titles, lands, money, or even positions of stature in society. But while one can inherit opportunity, and even be told of the standard of excellence that has existed in the past, it is always up to the individual to achieve it. We must strive toward it, work toward it, and never give up on it. To give up on achieving excellence is to show ingratitude to God. And while most of us didn't really inherit any of those aforementioned blessings, all of us can achieve the highest good no matter our post or position in this world.

Now don't misinterpret me here. I am not suggesting that we make an idol out of an ideal. I am merely stating that if our starting point with excellence is God, and our decision to achieve excellence is motivated by our gratitude for grace, then continually seeking the highest good is completely logical. That means the student in the band fulfills the role of band member by always seeking the highest good. The football player who didn't make the starting lineup doesn't sulk his way through a season but practices hard and serves his team because he is seeking the highest good. The stay-at-home mom who pulls off the impossible every day caring for a home and getting the kids to every practice does so seeking the highest good for her home and her family. The soldier, the teacher, the painter, the dentist, the doctor, and the mechanic are all seeking the highest good. The list could go on and on, but it will always come down to one thing: *We seek to achieve the highest good, a standard of excellence, because we are grateful that God gave the greatest good He could ever give to humanity—Jesus.*

Excellence is substance over shadow. In filling out our definition of excellence, we need to distinguish between what is substantive and what isn't, substance versus shadow. Let's be as clear as we can on this: excellence is not just some showy thing. It is not as simple as cropping out the unwanted or selecting just the right filter. In other words, excellence is not a façade. Such an approach is pretending excellence, but the moment you take a deeper look, it's lacking the substantive standard of achieving the highest good. It can easily be compared to an object that comes in between light and a surface, thus creating a shadow. The shadow doesn't weigh anything because it has no substance.

To fall short of a standard of excellence, only then to pretend, is a form of hypocrisy, which is really just another form of mediocrity. Excellence isn't just the appearance of something for a moment to make an impression. This shadowy or pretend excellence is like someone who always carries a book around but isn't really a reader. It's just a shadow. They are lacking substance, and if you were to ask them to summarize the last few books they read, they couldn't.

Pretend excellence is dangerous when you think about it. It creates a false impression, invites people to trust something that isn't substantial, and ultimately expresses to God: "I want the greatest good you can give me, but You can't have my highest good as an offering in response." I am reminded of when Jesus said, "Not everyone who says to me, 'Lord, Lord,' will enter the kingdom of heaven, but only the one who does the will of my Father in heaven" (Matt. 7:21).

My hope for all of us is that the joy of the Lord would so fill our hearts that we will be people of substance. That we will journey well because we have been well loved by God. That the appearance, the impression we give, is authentic, not pretend. And that is how you know you are a person of substance: when the outward appearance is a reflection of an inward reality.

People of excellence, excel. Now I'm going to let you in on a little secret that has existed for much of history. The people who make significant impacts and changes in their cultures are usually not the people born with the most amount of raw talent. The people who excel in culture are typically those who maintain a standard of excellence and are therefore, at times, willing to do what so many are unwilling to do. Like Rebekah in Genesis 24 who, when asked for a drink of water by a servant of Abraham, said, "I'll also draw water for your camels until they have had enough to drink" (v. 19). I have often heard of Rebekah's actions as the principle of *and then some.* She was asked for a drink, but she probably assumed the animals used for traveling must also be thirsty. She was willing to do more.

People who maintain a standard of excellence are unsatisfied accomplishing the least amount necessary to get through the day. This attitude of continually seeking the highest good is probably why so many people of excellence value setting goals. People set goals in all kinds of ways. Some are rigid, seeking to accompany each goal with a well-articulated time-management plan. Others seek to keep their goals in front of them so they will have visuals to serve as consistent reminders. In any case, people of excellence excel because they are striving toward a goal.

Several years ago at one of our Student Leadership University 301 conferences in London, we had the privilege of listening to a distinguished member of House of Lords in Parliament. He had spent much of his life focusing on helping organizations run efficiently in his country and was considered a thought leader on the subject. His entire talk was amazing, but I'll never forget one piece of advice he gave our students that day, "My dear friends from the States, I have been fortunate enough to work with hundreds of companies here in the UK, and I can tell you one thing for certain. Those who have five-year goals end up accomplishing exponentially more than those without any goals." It was so simple, yet it was so profound that I immediately wrote it down and have given it much thought ever since.

We wander in this world as pilgrims making our way home and seek to journey maintaining a standard of excellence. This standard means that we accomplish, we seek to achieve, out of a spirit of gratitude for the grace bestowed on us. And if we take this seriously, in our effort to achieve excellence, we set goals so that we have something to accomplish within the journey, as we maintain our eye on the ultimate prize of the journey.

Closing Charge for a People of the Highest Good

We are a people of the highest good.
We are a people made pilgrims because of
    God's greatest good.
And so we wander onward achieving
    because we have been approved.
We've been changed inward, so we move
    forward,

Achieving things that make the good Father
     proud,
Serving well because we have been captured
     by the wonder of the Savior.
Our journeys are not paved with good
     intentions
But accomplishments that stand as memor-
     ials to grace.
We are a people of action.
We set goals.
We dream dreams.
We articulate vision.
We waste not the moments at hand, for they
     will never be here again.
The journey is long, and shortcuts are for
     the naïve.
The standard that governs us cannot be
     downloaded or purchased.
The standard that governs can only be
     understood as a response, an offering.
And one that will be made time and
     again by those bound for the heaven
     country—
By those clothed in grace,
By those motivated by love,
By those determined to live well.
Why? One may ask . . .
Because grace—
Yeah, because grace understood demands
     more and never less.

The most mentioned theme and word throughout all of
Paul's writings is *grace*. His constant awareness of God's grace
compelled him to maintain a standard of excellence in all

things. This is something that could have easily consumed his thoughts as midnight was approaching. It is then a helpful endeavor to learn this standard of excellence, from such a great leader, so that whether we eat or drink or whatever we do, we may do it to the glory of God.

Ten O'clock
Sanctifying Failure and Redeemed Regret

During its day Rome was among the most metropolitan cities in the world. Certain parts of the city would stay active late into the twilight hours with entertainment of all kinds. Other parts would slow down like any street turned marketplace as everyone had gone home to see their families and rest before another day of bartering, buying, and selling. The streets around the Mamertine Prison were relatively quiet. From the belly of the beast that is the dungeon where Paul was chained, he could hear the occasional shuffling of sandals, possibly bits and pieces of a distant conversation of guards, and maybe the occasional dog barking. The flickering from the torches above ground weren't enough to disturb anyone attempting rest. It was as if the city above ground seemed to live unaware of the human beings rotting away beneath.

For the most part Paul had spent his day encouraged, thinking back on all the people and places, all the correspondence and conversation. It was overwhelming in the way a good movie can draw you in and make two and a half hours seem to fly by. So the moments of the day were for Paul, seeming to evaporate with ease ever since the converted guard had passed him the note at noon. His moments 'til midnight were rapidly approaching.

I can't help but wonder, though, if at some point this great man of God, now just a pilgrim almost home, allowed the darkness to affect his thinking and soul to some degree? After all, being an apostle didn't make him perfect, so he would have made mistakes, and he would have had struggles. Obviously he had his thorn in the flesh (2 Cor. 12:7), but there must have been other mistakes and struggles that were never recorded in his writings. We know, for example, that he struggled with anxiety about the churches he planted and the new believers he had seen convert. Did Paul struggle with depression somewhere on the other side of a beating, after a shipwreck, or during an imprisonment? Was he ever tempted to believe that maybe Jesus wasn't the Messiah? Did the ghosts of his past life, all the lives he had ruined before his conversion, ever come back to haunt him? Are we to believe that Paul never struggled in this sense? He may have been a saint, but this side of heaven he was also a sinner. And we would do well to think of him as human.

To see Paul this way demonstrates how the grace of Jesus really is sufficient. Let us view him as someone seeking to live a life of excellence and obedience to the faith. We may not always feel like we can relate to Paul, but I am sure he would look at our lives and certainly be able to relate to a people who struggle to some degree with failure and regret.

Every one of us deals with failure and regret, and Paul was no exception. The most obvious failure was his belief—before he was converted—that Jesus was a pretend Messiah who would disappear from the pages of history once His followers had been arrested and imprisoned. Yet from that failure Paul discovered the risen Lord and therein discovered his purpose. With two hours left to live, he could have easily traced the sovereign hand of God throughout his life just as much in his failure as in his successes. Therefore, ten o'clock is dedicated to the role of failure and regret in the pilgrim's journey.

Sanctifying Failure

Failure That Fails to Please God

There is a type of failure that is bad, and by bad I mean sinful. I know that may not seem like a grand revelation giving the definition of the term: "an act or instance of failing or proving unsuccessful; lack of success."[1] But not all failure is equal in the sight of God. Some failure can be good and edifying, which we will see in a moment. But one kind of failure detracts from living a full life. Some decisions leave us feeling empty, guilty, and longing for health. In my life I have experienced sanctifying and sinful failure, and the latter far too often.

I want to take a moment here and make sure something is beyond crystal clear. The failure that fails to please God is in fact sin. Paul wrote about this on multiple occasions:

> For all have sinned and fall short of the glory of God. (Rom. 3:23)

> For we know that our old self was crucified with him so that the body ruled by sin might be rendered powerless so that we may no longer be enslaved to sin, since a person who

has died is freed from sin. Now if we died with Christ, we believe that we will also live with him, because we know that Christ, having been raised from the dead, will not die again. Death no longer rules over him. For the death he died, he died to sin once for all time; but the life he lives, he lives to God. So, you too consider yourselves dead to sin and alive to God in Christ Jesus. (Rom. 6:6–11)

He made the one who did not know sin to be sin for us, so that in him we might become the righteousness of God. (2 Cor. 5:21)

Now those who belong to Christ Jesus have crucified the flesh with its passions and desires. If we live by the Spirit, we must also keep in step with the Spirit. (Gal. 5:24–25)

Theologian Wayne Grudem defines sin as "any failure to conform to the moral law of God in act, attitude, or nature."[2] Sin is any failure that fails to please God. My reason for stressing, or maybe overstressing, it here is that we seem to live in a world that tolerates every action, decision, perspective, lifestyle, and so on. We shrug off sin as though it were no big deal—even in the church. We often use euphemisms to soften the sound of our sin: words like *messy*, *imperfect*, and *in process*. While we are messy, imperfect, and in process, we must not forget that we are also sinful. And our sin displeases God. Paul makes clear, as we saw in the last chapter, that grace experienced should bid us to live with a sacred sense of responsibility—to live free from sin and all the entanglements that accompany such a lifestyle.

As we have already seen, Paul's greatest failure happened before his pilgrimage began. He believed Jesus to be a fake, a fraud, a pretend Messiah. He believed his job was to squash this movement before it ever gained momentum. But once he saw the light, literally, and the error of his worldview, everything changed. He realized the sinfulness of his sins and that he was wrong in his assessment of Jesus and subsequent actions. In short, Paul, before his conversion, was a complete failure. And then in one fateful moment he was transformed into a trophy of grace in God's family. But just because Paul was now a Christian, that didn't mean everyone else all of a sudden got a blessed case of amnesia! After all, he had earned a reputation. Some may even have doubted his conversion as a ruse to discover and imprison more Christ followers.

So the question becomes, How did Paul overcome this type of failure? Now, obviously God granted him significant favor. But I believe some practical principles are transferrable to anyone who is trying to overcome the type of failure that fails to please God.

How to Overcome Failure That Fails

STEP 1: WHEN ONE PERSON BELIEVES IN YOU

Remember Barnabas? We talked about him in an earlier chapter. The disciple from the island of Cyprus who sold his property and donated it to the apostles after the day of Pentecost. Barnabas was the guy that believed in Paul when everyone else thought there was no way such a conversion could be true: "When he arrived in Jerusalem, he tried to join the disciples, but they were all afraid of him, since they did not believe he was a disciple. Barnabas, however, took him and brought him to the apostles and explained to them how Saul had seen the Lord on the road and that the Lord had

talked to him, and how in Damascus he had spoken boldly
in the name of Jesus" (Acts 9:26–27). And when the church
in Jerusalem sent Barnabas to Antioch to help in the ministry
there, he decided to take the long way and stop by Tarsus
to pick up Paul along the way. He and Paul were a team for
many of the early years, accompanying each other on the first
missionary journey.

How did Barnabas ever become convinced of the genu-
ineness of Paul's conversion? Well, here's a novel idea—
maybe he was willing to get to know him! Maybe Barnabas
befriended the sinner Jesus saved while everyone else was
still scared of him. He was the saint that believed Saul was
a new creation when everyone else thought the whole thing
might be a trick. Barnabas chose to believe what God was
doing instead of seeing Paul for what he had done in the past.

No wonder Barnabas's name means "son of encouragement." He was a source of encouragement in Paul's life when
everyone else was skeptical. He believed first what everyone
else would come to know later. Oh how the world needs
some encouragers who spend their days . . .

> Believing in people everyone else has writ-
> ten off.
>
> Realizing it's never a risk to hope in some-
> one's redemption story.
>
> Befriending the sinner turned saint when
> others act like a saint turned sinner.
>
> Vouching for people that no one wants to
> trust.
>
> Partnering with the unlikely while others
> wait for them to prove what God has
> done.

Barnabas is such a great example of how one friendship can have such an enduring impact. And so we see that the first step in overcoming failure can happen when one person begins believing what we want everyone else to believe about us.

STEP 2: WHEN GOD'S GRACE IS LOUDER THAN OUR PAST SINS

As we have already seen, grace was the most mentioned word in all of Paul's writings. Furthermore, his testimony or conversion experience is shared three times in the book of Acts (chapters 9; 22; 26). So what are we to make of this emphasis on grace and the repetition of recounting his conversion in our study on overcoming failure? Could it be that the longer Paul lived and followed Jesus, the more prominent the theme of redemption became in his story? The more he journeyed the path of a pilgrim, the more people began to see him as someone wandering toward the heaven country.

Overcoming failure isn't something that just happens overnight. Be patient and steadfast. And as you endure, the work of God in you becomes more evident. As it becomes more evident, everyone else becomes more convinced. Now I'm not suggesting that we live to please the audience around us. I am simply saying that the redemption song of your life eventually drowns out the noise of your past, leaving all who observe evidence that can lead to only one verdict.

I'm not a good cook, but I'm halfway decent on the grill, and I have a smoker where I like to smoke chicken, brisket, turkey, and a few other meats. If you've ever had smoked meat, it's a flavor that makes your mouth water. In my years of grilling and smoking meat, I have learned if I want the meat to taste good, I needed to marinate it in the right marinade and be patient enough to let that marinade saturate the meat. The same process is true when overcoming failure. We need to marinate our lives in the change we want to become and be patient so that the change saturates our lives.

This is increasingly difficult in an age of technology that provides so much to us at such a fast pace. But overcoming failure doesn't occur at the same speed it takes to download an app. Overcoming takes patience and a willingness to let the rest of the world catch on to what we already know. But if you are willing to stay the course, there will be a moment when who you are becoming is more noticeable and memorable than all the mistakes of the past. Because at some point the grace of God drowns out the noise of our past sins.

STEP 3: WHEN THE FUTURE BECOMES MORE RELEVANT THAN THE PAST

The first two steps to overcoming failure lay the foundation for the third. There is a moment in the journey when your vision for the future is the most relevant thing about you. Paul was rejected in more towns and regions than received in those beginning days. And he had a knack for knowing when to escape by night because of a death threat to be carried out on his life. It's not like all the church plants and ministries in various cities just blossomed like flowers after a hard winter welcoming spring rains. Paul spent many years in some places tilling the ground again and again before it was receptive to the gospel and churches were planted and becoming healthy.

At some point Paul was no longer the Pharisee that got radically saved. Sure, that testimony was still true, but as his redemption song continued to ring forth, drowning out the noise of the past, vision of Paul's life became the most relevant thing about him. He was God's *chosen instrument* to be the great apostle to the Gentiles. This was his future, his calling. It was for this endeavor that he would exhaust himself over and over again. It is a simple yet beautiful process, isn't it? Barnabas believes, encourages, and takes the initiative to put Paul in the game, so to speak. They make a great team and begin serving together so much so that the grace of God in Paul's life drowns out the noise of his terrorist like reputation. Then, as the work of Christ becomes more and more apparent, the future vision of Paul's life to be an apostle to the Gentiles becomes more and more relevant.

Paul had experienced what so many desire in their own lives. He had overcome failure, the type of failure that fails to please God. I refuse to believe this three-step process is relevant to just one man who lived centuries ago. We seek to wander well through this broken world, but there may be a time when we make a mistake that can cost us our reputation, a job, or an important relationship. God's grace is so amazing in part because our failure that fails to please him doesn't have to be the final act in our journeys. Our stories don't have to end with our stupid decisions. Once we have petitioned King Jesus for forgiveness, we see in Paul a pathway back to being believable and trustworthy in our communities again. Restoration is possible and even probable when we imitate this pattern. Relationships can be restored, trust can be rebuilt, reputation can be regained, and a good and exciting future can be possible when we are willing to do things God's way.

Failure That Sanctifies and Thus Satisfies God

If you're reading this and are a millennial, born between 1980 and 1994, or part of Gen-Z, born between 1995 and 2010, then you probably have the mind-set that failure can be good. Failure doesn't necessarily mean a moral or ethical breakdown. In other words, there is a type of failure that isn't sin! We will call this "sanctifying failure." This is when we try to do something good, in accordance with the Scriptures, rightly motivated, but fail. This is a good type of failure that can mean we need to keep looking for the right solution. It can be a catalyst to good character, or it can just be the right warning sign to quit one endeavor and begin another.

I think God likes this kind of failure. I think it makes Him smile to see His sons and daughters using their imaginations, being obedient to the faith, and trying different ways to advance the cause of Christ. It's like a loving mother or father watching their daughter take her first steps. The baby can't walk far before she falls, but the parents aren't frustrated when she does; they're exuberant that she tried and that she made it as far as she did. This is a good kind of failure that can be edifying and even sanctifying. In fact, this type of failure moves us closer to God through its inevitable twists and turns.

Sanctifying failure . . .

> Stirs a deeper sense of dependency on God's authority and sovereignty.
>
> Can be good practice for a later success or door of opportunity.
>
> Eliminates options and thus narrows us in on the best possibility.

I have experienced this type of failure often in my life. I remember when I was a youth pastor in my early twenties trying to get my students excited about evangelism. I used Matthew 4:19 as our main passage. Jesus said, "Follow me . . . and I will make you fish for people." In an effort to create an environment that supported this emphasis, we painted the walls to look like we were underwater and themed the whole thing out with cast nets and so forth. But the icing on the cake was an idea I had that I was sure would galvanize the students to care about their lost friends. I took what little money we had in the budget and purchased a fish tank with the idea that every time someone made the decision to follow Jesus we would add a fish to the tank. Brilliant, right? Nope!

I had never owned a fish tank before and knew nothing about filters and oxygen levels and keeping a tank clean, much less keeping the fish alive. When I introduced this idea to our students, they thought it was great, and that day we put three fish in the tank to symbolize the three students who committed to following Jesus that month. By the next Sunday I had killed all three fish. From then on I was constantly cleaning the tank, flushing dead fish, and trying to remember how many I needed to replace before the next time the students would be back in our youth room. Then somehow I bought fish that would fight and kill one another and even feast on the dead carcasses. Needless to say, it was a complete train wreck. Some weeks it was the source of a bad smell and every week a cause of humor for my students. Questions like, "So, when we become Christians, you want us to turn into zombies and eat one another?" And, "Does all that algae on the sides of the tank represent sin in our friends' lives?" My favorite was the eighth-grader who waxed on and on about how we could die and be brought back to life as a different human being. The basis for his theological position was that he had seen me flush an orange fish and replace it with a black and gold one.

I look back on the whole fishers of men fiasco and to this day can't help but laugh at myself. But as I think about that experiment gone wrong, a complete failure, I don't think it displeased God. If anything I may have given Him a good laugh. And through it I learned something by trying and failing but not sinning. I found other creative methods to motivate students, and I learned to trust more in God's sovereignty. After all, students were still getting saved, and I can promise you it had nothing to do with my fish tank. So go ahead and get some good failures under your belt, the type of failures that edify, eliminate options, and cause you to trust God all the more because this type of failure is part of your sanctification and even satisfies the God we serve.

Redeemed Regret

I remember being a lowerclassman in high school and feeling the full weight of that awkward identity. Each day we sat in a large open cafeteria that was shaped like a long rectangle. Probably like every other high school on the planet, some people sat at tables based on grade, but most of us would take a seat acutely aware that where we sat said something about our status in the social hierarchy of the school. I never sat with the cool kids; truthfully, I never knew where to sit, and every day was a guess. It was a typical school in a country town. Certain people held a clout that placed them on a higher dimension of living than the rest of us. And because such a social hierarchy existed, something else called bullying was prevalent. At my school bullying was a spectator's sport during the forty-five minutes we had each day for lunch, and one kid got it worse than anyone else.

The bullies had a twisted way of coming up with stupid and demeaning nicknames for people who were the focus of their predatory behavior. Because of the rectangular shape of our lunchroom, the predators would sit at the end of the room where everyone had to pass when returning their empty trays and trash. As students drew near, they began to shout nicknames, get others to join in, hurl questions no human should hear, and occasionally threw food. It was a gauntlet of verbal, and certainly psychological, abuse.

One young lady—I think she was one grade below mine—seemed to receive a particularly cruel amount of their attention. She had frizzy hair and, like the rest of us in those awkward years, was still probably trying to grow into her body. Oftentimes in the ninth grade you can feel like a disproportionate human being. You know, where your arms and legs are uneven to the rest of you. Every day the ninth-grade awkward version of herself walked the gauntlet. It was bad. My skin crawled listening to the names and the taunts thrown her way day after day. It made me sick at my stomach. But she never cried. She never acknowledged the insults. She kept looking forward and, after returning her tray, went back to her seat.

I found out some time later that one night she tried to commit suicide. I guess she had had enough and couldn't walk that gauntlet of abuse one more time. At this point you may be thinking things like, *Where were the teachers?* Or, *Someone should have brought those jerks up on charges.* Those and other sentiments make complete sense. But when I think about the cafeteria abuse, my thoughts are different. I don't just point an accusatory finger at the bullies. Lots of other people, like me, sat and did nothing. While I didn't join in the heckling and name calling, I didn't intervene either. Sure, I had a list of reasons for not getting involved:

- I'm in the tenth grade and those are upperclassman. What on earth could I do to stop them!
- She isn't reacting. Maybe she's just letting it go.
- If I say or do something, then I'll become the object of their abuse.

The list could go on, but you get the point. Truthfully, I didn't even know the girl's name! In the end I was full of excuses: I was weak, scared, and basically a coward. And to this day I regret it. I regret not befriending her, not walking the gauntlet with her and whispering into her ear, "I'm with you. If they come after you, they'll have to come after us." I regret not confronting the bullies.

Regret is part of life.

There has never been a life lived, a journey taken, or a story told that didn't have some element of regret. I've heard some inspirational speakers proclaim to an audience "to live your life so there are no regrets." Such talk is foolery, naiveté, trickery, or maybe some of each. Just as failure is part of the journey, so is regret. We will all do things or not do things, say things or not say things, that we wished had gone differently. The question we have to wrestle through is, *What will we do with regret?* I once heard a friend say, "God doesn't erase our memories, but God will certainly heal our memories." So maybe the question is, How can God heal and redeem our regrets?

Three Possibilities for Regret

Possibility 1: Guilt—When Regret Is a Prison of Our Own Making

Because the past cannot be changed, the regret some people experience becomes a prison of guilt. When regret leads to guilt, we wallow away in the decay of bad decisions wondering if the padlock will ever be taken off this prison of our own making. Guilt can be such an impossible weight to shoulder. On the outside we may look like we are holding everything together, but on the inside we are like an abused child curled up in the corner of a dark room. And that's the thing with guilt; it forces you to become two different people. If guilt were a theatrical performance, then it would be a one-man show that forces you to play different parts.

People try to cope with guilt in many different ways. Many seek to punish or numb themselves in hopes of alleviating the guilt they feel in their conscience. Such activities include everything from self-harm to extreme physical exercise, from addiction to substance to becoming a workaholic. Some people throw themselves into a charity or some kind of service to others in an effort to work off the burden of guilt, like a debt that is owed. But if you have ever struggled with guilt—and we all have—then you know our best efforts can't remove the weight of it. That regret is still there, reminding us of our inadequacy and fueling the guilt all the more.

Possibility 2: Fear—When Regret Causes Us to Believe We Can't Succeed

The second possible outcome of regret is fear, which can be just as destructive to our souls as guilt. I am specifically talking about the type of fear that holds our future hostage. This happens when I regret something so much that fear and shame consume me and I am unable to move forward in life. The idea of fear robbing us of our future is as old as time itself. In Genesis 3, Eve engaged the serpent-devil in conversation, and both she and Adam ate the fruit of the tree that God had told them not to eat. We then see the fall of mankind into sin. Adam and Eve had rebelled against the explicitly stated desired will of God when He said: "And the LORD God commanded the man, 'You are free to eat from any tree of the garden, but you must not eat from the tree of the knowledge of good and evil, for on the day you eat from it, you will certainly die'" (Gen. 2:16–17).

Of course we know how the story goes: they both ate of the fruit and instead of having godlike power, their eyes were opened to their own inadequacy and shame. So they covered their nakedness with fig leaves and hid from God when He came walking in the garden. "So the LORD God called out to the man and said to him, 'Where are you?' And he said, 'I heard you in the garden, and I was afraid because I was naked, so I hid'" (Gen. 3:9–10).

Prior to this Adam and Eve had never experienced fear. In fact, God only wanted them to experience good things from Him, and fear wasn't on the list. Fear was the result of realizing and regretting a decision they had made that was contrary to what God had asked. Maybe we should think about it this way—the emotion God didn't want us to experience was the first emotion we did experience after we failed to follow His guidance.

Possibility 3: Freedom—When Regret Reminds Us to Live Redeemed

Guilt can imprison us, and fear can rob us of our future. Both are consequences of our own decision making and sinfulness. In short, regret can destroy our lives if we let it. But just as the story of Adam and Eve doesn't end with their rebellion, so our journeys don't have to end with our regrets. The hope of redemption first mentioned in the creation narrative (Gen. 3:15) is the only pathway to freedom from guilt and fear.

If you want freedom, you have to lay your regret at the feet of Jesus, repent of that past mistake that caused regret, and then repent for holding on to that regret and not living forgiven. Then, and only then, will we experience freedom. Freedom from regret, as a source of guilt and fear, happens when we believe God when He says:

> But now, apart from the law, the righteous-
> ness of God has been revealed, attested by
> the Law and the Prophets. The righteousness
> of God is through faith in Jesus Christ to all
> who believe, since there is no distinction.
> For all have sinned and fall short of the glory
> of God. They are justified freely by his grace
> through the redemption that is in Christ
> Jesus. (Rom. 3:21–24)

The gift of God's righteousness freely given to us by His grace is our only hope for freedom. It's as if we were slaves to our regrets, guilt, and fear, and He brought us out of slavery into freedom, that is to say He redeemed us by His blood. John Piper, when preaching on this text, said:

> God has not left us to deal with our guilt
> alone, but he has taken the initiative, while
> we were yet sinners (Romans 5:8), to seek
> our acquittal and to offer it to us freely. The
> glory of the gospel is that the one before
> whom we are guilty and condemned has
> himself undertaken to replace our guilt and
> his indignation with righteousness and rec-
> onciliation. This act of God which puts us
> in a right relationship to him where there
> is no more guilt and condemnation is called
> "justification."[3]

When we believe we have been *justified freely by His grace*, then the option of living in guilt and fear is no longer avail-able to us. We have thus been redeemed from the guilt and fear brought on by regrets, and they now serve as a memorial to God's grace in our lives. The cause of the regret can't be erased—it happened. But we can live forgiven and thus free. Regret now simply reminds us of the person we never want to be again; it reminds us of how we have been completely forgiven; it reminds us to live redeemed. It is no longer just "regret"; it is now a "regret redeemed."

As I mentioned earlier, I regret not standing up for the girl who was bullied in my lunchroom cafeteria in high school. I am forgiven, and that event, however unfortunate it was, now serves as a reminder of the type of person I never want to be again. It is a memorial of grace in my journey that now helps me continue onward, motivated to stand up for those who are marginalized. While we can't erase the darkness of the past, by God's grace the future can be bright with Technicolor opportunity to be salt and light.

Eleven O'clock
Life Imitates Story

Several years ago I was sitting at a café having a monthly coffee with a friend. We did our best to get together once a month to catch up on life, family, and whatever else was going on in our lives. About twenty minutes into our meeting, my phone rang. I typically try not to look at my phone during meetings, whether business or friendly, when I can help it. However, the phone, which I now had on vibrate, just kept buzzing and buzzing, so finally I looked down and saw that my younger brother had called three times in a row. This of course was cause for concern so I immediately excused myself and called him back.

I'll never forget the tone of his voice, the awkward silence before he tried to get sentences out, and the crackling sound words make when someone is holding back tears. Even though he was in Colorado and I was in Florida, the weight of the message he had to deliver bridged the gap, making it feel as if we were in the same room. "Brent, dad just had a stroke, and we are at the hospital in Colorado Springs. They are about to life-lift him to another hospital in Denver that is more suited to care for this sort of thing."

On my end of the phone, there was stunned silence. I was probably only quiet for a few moments, but during that time so many thoughts passed through my brain. *How could my dad have a stroke? He's in such great health—yesterday he told me he had been cross-country skiing. People who go cross-country skiing don't have strokes, do they? And he doesn't smoke or drink or eat a lot of red meat. I mean the guy seemed to be doing everything one would need to do to be healthy.* And then one thought took center stage: *Is he going to die?*

I didn't want to ask my brother that question, so instead I fumbled over my words, saying, "Is he . . . all right; I mean, is he . . . going to be OK?" My brother knew what I was asking and replied, "Brent, he is going to live. All I can tell you is that I am here, watching him and praying, and I just feel in my mind and heart that he is going to live." I replied, "OK man, then I'm on the next flight and will be there as soon as I can."

It was a blustery, gloomy, cold day when I landed in Denver, Colorado. The snow on the ground hadn't decided if it wanted to melt or just turn a slushy brown as I made my way through the city to the hospital. Before long I found my way to the parking lot, inside the hospital, and then took the elevator to the intensive care unit that specialized in people with brain injuries. It's hard for me to describe my first impressions when I walked into my dad's hospital room. The man who had carried me on his shoulders when I was a child, played with me in the backyard countless times, who had taught me to drive, and who had played in the pool with his grandkids, had been rendered completely paralyzed on the left side of his body. His sight had been reduced to blurry objects moving around him, and his hearing was likewise weakened.

I remember the first night I spent alone with him in his room so my mother could get some rest at a nearby hotel. In an effort to lighten the mood, I announced, "Hey Dad, boys' night in. What do you want to do?" I went on to suggest he could have me turn on a movie or show that he could listen to since his sight was still pretty bad; or maybe I could go get him some ice cream for dinner instead of whatever diet his doctor had him on. These suggestions caused him to chuckle a little bit only to go quiet for a few moments. He then said, "Brent, I haven't read my Bible in a week." At that moment a thousand memories simultaneously flooded my mind of seeing my dad every morning at the kitchen table with a hot cup of coffee and an open Bible. "Sure, Dad, I can read you your Bible. Where is it?" He then smiled—that is, he smiled with the right side of his face since the left was paralyzed. "I didn't have time to pack!" he chuckled. The man had gone to death's door but not lost his sense of humor. "Why don't you read me yours," he said.

I took out my Bible and a devotional book I was working through entitled Christ in Us by Ian Thomas. It focused each day's readings on the sufficiency of Christ. I turned to where I had left off the previous day, flipped over and read from Colossians 3:11 (NLT), "In this new life, it doesn't matter if you are a Jew or a Gentile, circumcised or uncircumcised, barbaric, uncivilized, slave, or free. Christ is all that matters, and he lives in all of us."

Now, I don't often get emotional, but when I finished reading the text and the words of Mr. Thomas, I closed my Bible and the devotional book. Then I looked across the room at my dad, who seemed to be leaning his head farther back than usual and was quietly staring at the ceiling. I stood to my feet, walked over, and leaned down and whispered into his ear, "Dad, what are you thinking about?" He responded, "I think . . . I think . . . I think it is good."

"What's good, Dad? I'm a bit confused."

He responded, "Didn't you read it!? Don't you know it!? Jesus is here and Jesus is good!"

Honestly in that moment I was struggling to see how Jesus is good. The thoughts that ran through my head weren't exactly positive. He may never walk again, drive a car again, put both arms around his wife again. He would never go to a theme park and ride rides with his grandkids again. In that moment I was consumed with all that he would never do again, but in that moment he was consumed with how *Christ is all that matters, and He lives in all of us.*

I had spent my entire life looking up to my dad. He led me to Jesus, discipled me, prayed for me when I wanted to go into ministry, and helped me write my first sermon. He had lived a life that honored Jesus, but the great prize of his journey was not found in what could be accomplished but rather a presence that could be experienced. I had spent my entire life as a child and now as an adult looking up to my dad, but it wasn't until I looked down at him in the midst of his most difficult days that I awakened to what he had been trying to teach me all along: *God's provision for my life is God's enduring presence in my life.*

The Pilgrim's Story and a Life Worth Imitating

When I think about my dad's journey—which by the way is far from over—I see a story worth imitating. I see someone wandering well and making his way to the heaven country. Some years later he continues to make incredible progress. In those first weeks following the stroke, the neurologist said he had less than a 15 percent chance of ever walking again; today he walks. While he no longer preaches and pastors a church, he is heavily involved in my home church where he fulfills a variety of ministry roles. And just recently we went to a theme park he had taken his grandkids to before his stroke, and he again rode rides and laughed with his grandkids. But while there are so many milestones to celebrate, milestones have never been the ultimate prize. Jesus is my dad's ultimate prize, which may be why he spends an hour every day just reading the Bible and talking to his Savior. When I think of a pilgrim's story that is a life worth imitating, I look no further than a man who lives with severe disabilities every day and probably knows better than I ever will the words of Jesus to Paul: *"My grace is sufficient for you, my power is made perfect in weakness"* (2 Cor. 12:9).

It is now eleven o'clock, and even though Paul didn't have a wristwatch, he was well aware of the scarcity of time he had left. By this moment, on this last day, he had surveyed so much in his life and journey. Now more than ever, everything about his pilgrimage felt contained in a narrative. Sitting in the darkness of a dungeon, alone with these thoughts, alone with his feelings, he was more convinced than he had ever been that this pilgrimage was worth taking. He would be more than happy to journey another ten thousand miles, get shipwrecked time and again, get beaten over and over—all if it meant he was able to spend those moments pleasing Jesus. A survey of his story leaves us with the sense that Paul would have gladly suffered several more lifetimes in prison if it meant Jesus was his cellmate. But while he would gladly suffer through another pilgrimage, what Paul longed for was his eternal home in heaven. Paul didn't have long left in this world, but I have to believe whatever time he did have was to be spent courageously at the feet of Jesus. This is never more evident than when he wrote:

> For we know that if our earthly tent we live in is destroyed, we have a building from God, an eternal dwelling in the heavens, not

made with hands. Indeed, we groan in this
tent, desiring to put on our heavenly dwell-
ing. . . . So we are always confident and know
that while we are at home in the body we are
away from the Lord. For we walk by faith,
not by sight. In fact, we are confident, and we
would prefer to be away from the body and
at home with the Lord. Therefore, whether
we are at home or away, we make it our aim
to be pleasing to him. (2 Cor. 5:1–2, 6–9)

The pilgrim's story should be well lived and thus worth
imitating. On a separate occasion he would tell the believers
in Corinth that they could imitate him as he imitated Christ
(1 Cor. 11:1). Paul sought for his life to imitate the story that
God is telling, which has redemption as its theme and Jesus
as its central figure. Therefore, in living out a narrative that
has redemption and the Redeemer as the central theme and
figure, Paul's life became imitable.

At this point we have studied and seen so much of Paul's
story. The following are a handful of observations about
Paul's journey through the lens of a story:

- His was a story that had redemption as
  the theme and the Redeemer as the hero.
- The twists and turns didn't bother him
  because he took great joy in the sufficiency of Christ in all things.
- He sought to step through doors of
  opportunity and accomplish God's
  vision for his life, all while cherish-
  ing his fellowship with Jesus above all
  accomplishments.

- He desired for God to be obvious in his story whether he was eating and drinking or preaching and church planting.
- Paul realized that glorifying God is not about the size of our accomplishments but the degree of our obedience to the faith.
- Paul believed his story was meant to help others tell their story (i.e., Timothy, Titus).
- He lived aware that because of God's grace the beginning of the story would not determine the end of the journey.

What's the Manuscript of Your Life Going to Look Like?

Oscar Wilde, a successful Irish poet and playwright, famously wrote in the late 1800s that "life imitates art far more than art imitates life." From everything I've read, Mr. Wilde was incredibly talented and smart, but I think a more accurate statement is, *Life imitates story, and all stories find their meaning and definition in the grand narrative of the gospel story.* Think about it—we are able to recognize good and evil, the hero and the villain, because God's story has already provided us a mental map and model of these elements. Whenever you watch the next superhero movie that hits the big screen, a handful of things will be true:

- The hero will discover or grow in the knowledge of his/her superpower.
- The hero will then realize personal responsibility, the existence of a villain,

and a mission he is to accomplish (good
versus evil).

- The hero will do battle with the villain,
the antihero, and will be willing to sacrifice his life for the greater good.

- The hero will appear to die or be seriously wounded, only to resurrect for the
climactic ending of the film or trilogy
of films.

Hmm. All that sounds like it resembles another hero.
Who could it be?

That's right, comic-book-put-to-movie fans everywhere.
We have Captain America and Superman because we first
had Jesus (I mentioned both so as not to offend team Marvel
or team DC Comics). Jesus is the ultimate hero that actually
saves; all other heroes can only make sense of their hero-ness
because Jesus has demonstrated and thus defined the meaning of *hero*. And this doesn't just apply to the hero element
of storytelling. All the different elements of all the different
stories, whether they be the journey that is our lives or something we watch to entertain us, find their meaning because
of the gospel story that is in the Bible.

Life imitates story because the Creator designed life to be
a narrative about a journey. We resonate with stories because,
whether we realize it or not, we are all storytellers who at
this moment are writing the autobiographies of our souls.[1]
Therefore the question becomes, What's the manuscript of
your life going to look like?

You may remember from literature class in school that a
story has five basic components: the characters, the setting,
the plot, the conflict, and the resolution. Therefore, the narrative that is our journey could be . . .

- Characters: The characters in our stories include the pilgrim and those whom the pilgrim associates with throughout his/her journey. Of course, the most important character is the hero, Jesus, who rescues us from our sin and sets us on a journey to the heaven country.
- Setting: The setting is God's creation that is completely broken as a result of the characters' decision to rebel against their Creator's desired will. In other words, the setting is the result of sin. Each character must realize personal responsibility for the world being broken.
- Plot: The plot or story line is that God redeems the characters through the work of Christ on the cross. Then each character or pilgrim is on a journey to make his way through this broken world toward the heaven country. As each pilgrim journeys through this world, he makes the world better through gospel ministry and demonstrates the hope for all characters who place their faith and trust in Jesus.
- Conflict: The conflict is that even though we are redeemed, we still struggle with the flesh and sinful desires: the consequences of living in a broken world and a spiritual battle often referred to as spiritual warfare.
- Resolution: The resolution is that God has provided for us a new setting, a new creation, that is heaven. We will live in

complete harmony with God and all that
the heaven country is forevermore.

This may be an oversimplification, but it further demonstrates the Bible to be a grand narrative—a story that
actually happened, that is inspired by God and thus alive
and thoroughly truthful. Furthermore, and to expand on the
story line of Scripture, the Bible could be understood in four
parts, or plot movements: creation, the fall, redemption, and
restoration.

Now watch this. You've probably picked up on how
the autobiography of our souls should have redemption as
its central theme and Jesus Christ as the central character.
The reason for this is simple: in the Scripture the theme of
redemption is given more attention and airtime than any
other theme. If the Bible is the greatest story, the story that
gives all others meaning and expresses God's desired will for
us, then it gives my story meaning. And if the work of Christ
is the central theme in God's story, then it should be the central theme of mine.

God's story gives mine meaning and direction. My story
minus the work of Christ just ends with me and the forever
consequences of my rebellion. My story minus Jesus means
no pilgrimage, no journey, and no heaven country. We can
then say that if redemption isn't the theme of our story, it is
probably not a story worth telling. But, my fellow pilgrims,
if redemption is the theme of our stories, not only are our
stories worth telling; they are worth imitating!

Is Your Life Imitable?

Let's do a little thought experiment. Pretend that a big theater production wanted to make a stage show out of your life.

Now the production company wants to make sure they get the story right and are going to spare no expense in an effort to showcase the life you have lived thus far. Of course, the first thing they need is a script. So an entire department of people go to work researching, piecing together, and storyboarding the moments of your life. After months of work, a manuscript is produced, characters are cast, and a stage is built including state-of-the-art props, sound, and lighting. On opening night the theater is packed because the marketing department has never failed to fill the seats. The sound of hundreds of separate conversations fills the lobby and theater. Soon thereafter the houselights flicker to signal everyone to take their seats. In a matter of minutes, almost a thousand people are sitting in their finest clothes, with programs in hand, anticipating a good night at the theater. The orchestra starts to play, the curtains open, and the show commences.

If the show went on about your life, what impact would it have on the audience? Would the central theme of redemption be undeniable? Would they see a character seeking to make God obvious in the big and small events of life? Is the character loving friends and enemies? Would they see conflict and a character experiencing Christ's sufficiency? Would they see shades of glory, a longing for eternity? Would it be a series of loosely connected events or a journey that had a well-defined beginning and a clear destination? What would the audience take away from the story of your life put under a spotlight for all to see?

The question that really answers all the other questions is this: *Is your life imitable? If others were to imitate your story, would they find themselves on the journey of a lifetime following Jesus and wandering well toward the heaven country?*

It really is a sobering question to ponder. I'm grateful that I've had a father who has shown me what the journey looks like. I'm grateful for Paul who told a story with his life that has helped countless others tell theirs.

Like my father and Paul, it's likely that someone has shown you the journey, the pilgrimage, the way homeward. Be for others what someone has been for you. Journey in such a way that your life gives others hope. Be the example that can be imitated, and tell a story that helps others tell theirs.

Midnight

Finished . . . Begin

Midnight was rapidly approaching.

Soon a rope would be lowered into the Mamertine Prison, and Paul would be lifted out of the filthy and unsanitary conditions he had come to know so well. I wonder, as he was being hoisted out of the dungeon, if he looked back down, while gripping the rope with old-man strength, at the temporary home he had made with the criminals of this world. I wonder if he tearfully looked back into the eyes of felons who had become friends, offering a prayer or word of encouragement. He would never see them again in this world.

For now he would be led away by a team of executioners whose existence and vocation reflected the darkness and disdain Nero felt toward Christianity. It would be a short distance until they came to the place, a place where unspeakable things happen. Someone would rip what was left of his rotting clothes from his neck to his waist. He possibly would have been beaten one last time with rods, an all-too-familiar occurrence that never felt familiar. His hands would have been tied, and he would have been dropped to his knees next to a pillar, where his neck could be fully exposed. Finally, with one swift movement of a sword, in a well-trained and experienced hand, Paul's life would come to an end.

The great historian John Pollock comments so gracefully on this event when he writes: "No executioner was going to lose him the conscious presence of Jesus; he was not changing company, only the place where he enjoyed it. Better still, he would see Jesus. Those glimpses—on the Damascus Road, in Jerusalem, at Corinth, on the sinking ship; now he was going to see Him face-to-face, to know even as he had been known."[1]

Death

We don't often talk about death in our culture. Or more accurately, we don't discuss how to die well. But midnight comes for us all. It is a question of being prepared for the chimes of the striking clock. In an age of advancing medicine and technology, the day and hour of our passing is as much a mystery as it ever has been. While at times it may be delayed, its arrival is entirely inevitable. For some death may be welcomed in the midst of intolerable suffering; for others, cruel in its seemingly early arrival. Some are able to see death approaching them from off in the distance like a slow-moving ocean liner, while others are blindsided.

In the end Paul knew his death was imminent. Reading 2 Timothy, we see that he seems to be at rest in the clarity that midnight would be here soon:

> For I am already being poured out as a drink offering, and the time for my departure is close. (2 Tim. 4:6)

I have fought the good fight, I have finished
the race, I have kept the faith. (2 Tim. 4:7)

Make every effort to come to me soon.
(2 Tim. 4:9)

Paul lived well, and now Paul would die well.

From One Side of the River to the Other

A young Methodist pastor was once called to the bed-
side of a dying elderly woman who had only a few hours
left to live. The young minister, with little experience, had
never been given such an assignment as comforting and
praying with someone who was dying. As he made his way
to the woman's home, he tried to remember his seminary
training, the right things to say and the right Bible verses
to quote. As the pastor nervously walked into her room, he
was immediately surprised at how relaxed and joyful the
woman appeared. In his attempt to minister to the woman,
he expressed how sorry he was for her suffering and that she
had to die. The elderly saint looked back at the young pastor
with an expression that communicated the young man's sad-
ness was considerably misplaced. Before the pastor could go
on, she interrupted and cheerfully said, "Why, God bless you,
young man, there's nothing to be scared about. I'm just going
to cross over Jordan in a few minutes, and my Father owns
the land on both sides of the river."[2]

I have never heard a more accurate description of death.
Death is like crossing a river. It is arriving at the destination
that was the point of the pilgrimage all along. In a world
where everyone is trying to prevent death, the pilgrim can
be the rare breed that is unafraid to die. That is not to say
pilgrims seek death. Dying well occurs when living well is

extended to the final moments of the journey. The key is for each of us to live like we are going to die well. And while death may mean our arrival to the heaven country, thus ending this journey, it does not mean that the story is over. In fact, when the pilgrimage ends, the story of our lives is really only beginning.

C. S. Lewis compared this life to a title page or prologue of a book. If he is correct, then our pilgrimage to the heaven country is but the title page to eternity, to a story still in its beginning when it crosses over the Jordan.

Paul was about to cross over that river. He was not long for this world, and I can't help but imagine how, at midnight, his thoughts turned to the glorious and gruesome death of his Savior. Jesus had died at the hands of Roman soldiers; now Paul would suffer a similar fate by similar hands. The grace of Jesus had been the great theme of his writings. It had been with him through years of prison and ten thousand miles of journeys. Now it would be with him in his dying moments. Or, as John Newton penned in 1779 as part of the great hymn "Amazing Grace," "Grace will lead me home."

Surely the words he had written in Philippians 3:10 came to mind, "My goal is to know him and the power of his resurrection and the fellowship of his sufferings, being conformed to his death." Paul ultimately wanted to know Christ and experience the power of His resurrection and fellowship of His sufferings. This means he wanted to be identified with Christ's crucifixion and resurrection. The power of Christ's resurrection speaks to the assurance that every believer has concerning immortality as the triumph over sin because: "He made the One who did not know sin to be sin for us, so that we might become the righteousness of God in Him."[3] As one theologian put it, fellowship of His sufferings is "the thought that when the Christian has to suffer, he is in some strange way sharing the very suffering of Christ and is even filling up that suffering (2 Cor. 1:5; 4:10–11; Gal. 6:17; Col. 1:24). To suffer for a faith is not a penalty, it is a privilege, for thereby we share the very work of Christ."[4]

As Paul was being led to his death, as he was moments away from crossing over into the heaven country, he was again willing to suffer for his faith and thus share in the work of Christ. Surely he would have been comforted by the image of Jesus dying on the cross while being guided away to his own Calvary. In thinking about suffering one last time, I wonder if he recalled some of the final words of Christ from the cross and if those comforting words from the lips of the Messiah aided him in dying well.

Jesus Teaches Us How to Die Well

Jesus made seven statements while hanging on the cross from nine in the morning until He breathed His last at three in the afternoon. In those seven statements, four audiences were identifiably addressed: the mob in front of the cross that included everyone from Roman soldiers to members of the Sanhedrin, the criminals hanging on either side of Him, His mother and friends, and finally His Father in heaven. In identifying Christ's message to these four audiences, we are given the greatest example of how to die well.

Jesus Died Extending Grace to the Undeserving

The mob mentality ran deep that day, full of senseless and prideful emotions. Just a handful of verses prior, the crowd standing before Pilate cried out "Crucify! Crucify him!" (Luke 23:21). Jesus had been scourged and beaten, a crown of thorns had been placed on His head, and a purple robe had been placed on His back. He stood next to Pilate and

before the crowd a bloody—dare we say unrecognizable—
mess of a human being. Yet the amount of gore and torment
He had endured thus far wasn't enough. They wanted more.
They wanted Him to be punished for a crime He never committed, and they wanted that punishment to be crucifixion.

Crucifixion was a common form of capital punishment
from the sixth century BC until it was banned by Constantine
in 337.[5] Even still it was considered a grotesque and inhumane
way to die and certainly the most cruel and painful way the
Romans could put someone to death. In fact, it was so barbaric that by law a Roman citizen could not be crucified.

So now Jesus is nailed to a cross through His wrists and
feet. And there suspended between heaven and earth, the
crowd mocked him from nine a.m. until noon. In that time
all stood guilty mocking the Suffering Servant:

- The crowd in front of the cross (Luke
  23:35)
- The soldiers who nailed him to the cross
  (Luke 23:36)
- The religious leaders who mocked and
  scoffed at him on the cross (Matt. 27:41;
  Luke 23:35)
- The criminals crucified on either side of
  him (Matt. 27:44)
- Even those who were passing by on the
  road (Matt. 27:39)

And what is the one thing they all have in common? In
a word, *ignorance*! They were ignorant concerning their own
sin and ignorant in that they didn't recognize Jesus to be the
Messiah, who at that moment was making a way for their
salvation. In this sea of ignorance, we have the first word
from Christ on the cross. Jesus cries out a prayer to God

that demonstrates patience and shows us the possibility of showing grace, even to the most undeserving. In Luke 23:34, "Jesus said, 'Father, forgive them, because they do not know what they are doing.'" To the crowd who had cried for His blood, Jesus was now extending grace.

The emphasis of Jesus' prayer is on forgiveness. This doesn't mean the crowd would not be held responsible for their current sins, but rather Jesus was praying to His Father in heaven to be patient and . . .

> Permit My sacrifice by way of crucifixion to continue.
> Allow Me to be the debtor so they can become free.
> Withhold your wrath and delay punishment for their sin until My sacrifice makes their redemption possible.

Jesus is showing us that forgiveness cannot be understood divorced from sacrifice. Forgiveness is authoritatively in the hands of God. No human could ever forgive his or her own sin. Ultimately through Jesus our Mediator, we see God's enduring love and commitment to redeem a people unto Himself. That is why Jesus' first word from the cross focused on forgiveness.

So, how does this inform and impact the pilgrim's thinking concerning the end of the journey? Jesus serves as a perfect model of how to forgive well. The people who journey well in this life are those who travel light, not lugging around resentment and bitterness. We should be encouraged by our Lord's example to forgive quickly and completely, to wander toward the heaven country free from the entanglements of unforgiveness so that when we take that final breath, we do so having extended grace to any and all who may have wronged us. This is why, after Paul describes to Timothy that everyone had deserted him, he immediately wrote, "May it not be counted against them" (2 Tim. 4:16). Paul wanted to finish his race knowing he had forgiven well. Because those who die at peace with God are those who have extended grace, even to the undeserving.

Jesus Died Giving Hope to the Hopeless

Our lives hinge on defining moments. The second statement from Jesus was one such moment for the criminal on the cross. While the events preceding the criminal's crucifixion aren't completely known to us, many historians have speculated that they were most likely following a false messiah named Barabbas. That's right, sports fans, the same Barabbas that was set free at the trial before Pontius Pilate.[6] Barabbas was a prisoner, a robber, and a revolutionary who wanted to overthrow the Roman government at any cost. He had most likely committed murder in the name of revolution. Thus he would have had followers that viewed him as a messiah-like figure, one who would save and liberate the Jewish people. Governor Pilate offered a choice, which was consistent with a custom during Passover, to release a prisoner to the crowd. The choice was between Jesus and Barabbas, and the crowd chose to set the murderer free.

> Pilate asked them, "What should I do then with Jesus, who is called Christ?"
> They all answered, "Crucify him!"
> Then he said, "Why? What has he done wrong?"
> But they kept shouting, "Crucify him!" (Matt. 27:22–23)

Fast-forward several hours, and the criminal, who had most likely followed the wrong messiah in his adult life, is now conversing with the true Messiah who at that moment was saving and liberating His people. From His birth to His death, Jesus was always caring for the outsider, the over-looked, and the least likely of candidates to be recipients of His grace. Jesus had a great habit of befriending those on the fringes of society.

In the beginning of His life, it was the shep-herds outside the city keeping their flocks.

And then throughout His ministry, Jesus could be found calling lowly fisherman to be followers and thus start a movement—

Touching and healing a leper who was liv-ing on death's door,

Bringing back to life the only son a mother would have,

Redeeming an immoral woman with a deplorable reputation,

Being a friend of sinners and even sharing meals with them,

Seeking out a tax collector who found ref-uge in a tree for fear of his life,

And yes, in the end, offering forgiveness and salvation to the criminal who had fol-lowed the wrong messiah.

To the criminal without hope, Jesus offers a heavenly home. Upon recognizing that Jesus had done nothing wrong and that he and his fellow criminal were receiving the right punishment for their actions, he makes one request: "'Jesus, remember me when you come into your kingdom!' And he said to him, 'Truly I tell you, today you will be with

me in paradise'" (Luke 23:42–43). The criminal "knocked
once, sought once, asked once, dared everything, and found
everything."[7]

I love the way Fulton Sheen described this criminal's
conversation with the Savior:

> A dying man asked a dying man for eter-
> nal life; a man without possessions asked a
> poor man for a Kingdom; a thief at the door
> of death asked to die like a thief and steal
> Paradise. One would have thought a saint
> would have been the first soul purchased
> over the counter of Calvary by the red coins
> of Redemption, but in the Divine plan it was
> a thief who was to escort the King of kings
> into Paradise.[8]

I love the image of our Lord entering heaven accompanied by a criminal who had spent his adult life following a
false messiah. That is a picture saturated with hope. I love that
Jesus cared for the obviously overlooked in society and that
one such creature was first to cross the Jordan after Christ
had breathed His last.

Ours is a journey filled with hope. Even when everything in the world feels more broken than usual, we sojourn
onward hoping in what we know and will one day see.
Therefore, the journey we take should be a testimony of
hope for all. Not just for those who seem most deserving or
those who are easy to reach out and love. But rather, our lives
should demonstrate to those that everyone else has ignored
and overlooked that hope has a name, and it is Jesus.

Oh that we would die having spent our lives climbing
into the ditch where the hurting and half dead of this world
make their homes. You know, with the kind of people the

priests and Levites bypass as unworthy of their time and energy. But make no mistake; we aren't seeking to rescue people on the fringes of society. Because we know how poor a substitute we are for the real Savior. Nonetheless, as we follow the example of Jesus, the people on the fringes of society actually become our friends. It is a two-way-street relationship between people who equally value one another. And through these relationships, people who others have bypassed begin to see hope.

Those who have wandered and finished the journey well have climbed into their fair share of ditches. They've dined with sinners and fellowshipped with outcasts. They have discovered the beauty of what seems to be unlikely friendship to the average bystander. Because there, in the ditches of this world, they have discovered a camaraderie when most see only uncomfortable situations to be avoided. They have witnessed the power of hope taking center stage in someone's life who was, well, hopeless.

Jesus Died Caring and Providing Community for His Heartbroken Family and Friends

Parents should never outlive their child, and certainly parents should never have to watch their child die. Both of these unfortunate events were true concerning the mother of our Lord.

Standing by the cross watching her child die for crimes He did not commit, she must have recalled the words of Simeon some thirty-three years earlier when she and Joseph had taken their son to be presented at the temple: "Indeed, this child is destined to cause the fall and rise of many in Israel and to be a sign that will be opposed—and a sword will pierce your own soul—that the thoughts of many hearts may be revealed" (Luke 2:34–35). Those words—*a sword will pierce your own soul*—must have become as real as the ground beneath her feet. The prophecy was accurate. She, at that moment, felt a pain beyond the ability of words to describe. The first time we see Mary in the book of John, she is preparing for a wedding (John 2:1–11), and now she would be preparing for a funeral.

Visualize in your mind's eye a dying Savior in excruciating pain reaching out to comfort His earthly mother:

> Standing by the cross of Jesus were his mother, his mother's sister, Mary the wife of Clopas, and Mary Magdalene. When Jesus saw his mother and the disciple he loved standing there, he said to his mother, "Woman, here is your son." Then he said to the disciple, "Here is your mother." And from that hour the disciple took her into his home. (John 19:25–27)

In this short and poignant statement, we see that Jesus was concerned that her heart must have been breaking inside her chest, that her physical well-being needed to be secure after His death, but also that at that moment she needed Him to be a heavenly Savior more than an earthly Son. In this statement we vividly see the care of a firstborn Jewish Son, and simultaneously the heart of the Savior concerned for the spiritual well-being of the world.

If a dying Paul looked to a dying Savior for an example to be emulated and words that would bring comfort, he must have recalled Jesus' words to His mother. It must have made him feel encouraged and reassured that he had focused so much time on Timothy, who would receive his last letter. Jesus had cared for those closest to Him in His dying hours, and so had Paul.

Jesus' words to His mother and John addressed Mary's emotional, physical, and spiritual needs. It was a holistic kind of care and a great example to Paul—so it should be for us. The pilgrim finishes well when he or she has sought to care for those who still have a journey ahead of them. By that I mean we take a holistic approach to care for those relationally closest to us before going home to the heaven country. It may sound like a bit of a paradox, but we die well when we help those we love to live well in our absence.

Jesus Died Being Faithful and Obedient to His Father in Heaven

In Jesus' final words before breathing His last breath, to His Father in heaven He offered faithfulness and obedience. Jesus died pleasing God and accomplishing all that was necessary to make salvation possible. Every once in a while it helps us to look back in history for profound explanations of such important statements as the one Christ made before dying: "It is finished" (John 19:30). With that in mind, the fourth-century church father Augustine wrote:

> When Jesus therefore had received the vinegar, He said, "It is finished." What, but all that prophecy had foretold so long before? And then, because nothing now remained that still required to be done before He died, as if He, who had power to lay down His life and to take it up again, had at length completed all for whose completion He was waiting, "He bowed His head, and gave up the ghost." Who can thus sleep when he pleases, as Jesus died when He pleased? Who is there that thus puts off his garment when he pleases, as He put off His flesh at

His pleasure? Who is there that thus departs when he pleases, as He departed this life at His pleasure? How great the power, to be hoped for or dreaded, that must be His as judge, if such was the power He exhibited as a dying man![9]

Augustine is emphatically emphasizing that Jesus was powerful enough to accomplish His task as the sacrifice, thus fulfilling His role as Messiah. Jesus, who was all man, all God, and all one, had used His power to please God. Nothing demonstrates this more so than the words "It is finished."

Jesus had accomplished His atoning work for the sins of the world. Our relationship with God had been destroyed in the garden in Genesis 3, but the death of Jesus made possible a new relationship with God. Every sinner accumulates a debt or punishment to be paid for his or her rebellion. God hates sin and cannot tolerate it in His presence, hence our expulsion from the garden. But in Christ, God's wrath toward our sin is appeased. This is why Paul writes in Romans 5:9, "Since we have now been declared righteous by his blood, will we be saved through him from wrath." We each owe a debt that we could never pay. So when Jesus uttered the words "It is finished," He was saying that our debt has been paid. Jesus has offered compensation with His blood to God on our behalf. That is why it's called grace and why our salvation could never be earned, but rather was accomplished for us by another.

Jesus died having finished the task, having pleased God the Father, and having made a way for us back into right relationship with God. To every pilgrim wandering toward the heaven country, our ultimate goal should be to cross the Jordan having pleased God with our lives. To die well we should seek to live well, or as has been stated continually throughout this book, journey well.

The entire point of the pilgrimage is to please God. And while no pilgrim can predict the moment the chimes of midnight will strike, every pilgrim can live obediently to the faith and thus die at peace with God. So let us say it this way: Jesus teaches us to finish having accomplished what you were put on Earth to do. He shows us that fulfilled purpose is a fulfilled life.

Jesus taught us how to die well by . . .

> Extending grace to the undeserving.
>
> Giving hope to the hopeless.
>
> Caring and providing for heartbroken family and friends.
>
> Being faithful and obedient to His Father in heaven.

In His death we see our life, but in His death we also see how to finish the journey well. Jesus' sacrifice made a way back to God, but it also serves as the greatest example of how to cross over the Jordan. In Christ's death we see how to cross over to the other side, where a new story awaits.

I alluded earlier to the ever-quotable C. S. Lewis. He taught us in the conclusion of his final installment of The Chronicles of Narnia that life and all its adventures are but a title page for eternity. That eternity is the "Great Story which no one on earth has read: which goes on for ever: in which every chapter is better than the one before."[10] Paul was well aware, possibly more so at midnight than any other time, that an even greater adventure was about to begin, "For me, to live is Christ and to die is gain" (Phil. 1:21).

Paul lived as a citizen of heaven making his way along this earthly pilgrimage. He lived aware that the best was yet to come. Thus on his final day in chains, he sought to redeem

the moments 'til midnight. We have imagined that he accomplished this by recalling such subjects as humility, gifting
and purpose, loneliness and friendship, heavenly thinking,
godly living, unity among the saints, belief in the seemingly
impossible, communication, a standard of excellence, failure
and regret, life as an imitable story, and how to finish well.
The thoughts he left behind, which constitute so much of
the New Testament, serve as relevant and sacred artifacts to
live well before God so that we might finish this life pleasing
Jesus . . . only to begin a greater story that has no end.

Midnight had finally arrived. There were no more
moments to experience on this side of the journey. The
pilgrimage had come to an end, but a greater story was just
beginning. Paul had finished . . . Paul would now begin. And
therein lies the glorious outcome for all pilgrims wandering
their way homeward—when we finish, it's really just the
beginning.

So to every pilgrim young and old,

Journey well in grace and purpose.

Live rich in community and friendship.

Keep your head in the clouds while
you walk the road less traveled.

Wear the wardrobe of grace because
you are holy and beloved.

Enjoy togetherness and celebrate unity
as the fruit of gospel-centeredness.

Believe every day that with God all things are possible.

Converse about the meaningful in a creative manner.

Sojourn with a standard of excellence
sourced in a healthy view of God.

And when you fail, fail well, and let
all your regrets be redeemed.

Tell a story with your pilgrimage
that is worth imitating.

Live well and cross the Jordan, knowing that
when you finish, it is only the beginning.

About the Author

Brent Crowe is a thought-provoking visionary and communicator who has a passion to present the life-changing message of the gospel. Brent uses humor and real-life situations to relate to people at the heart of their struggles. The roles of husband, father, minister, evangelist, author, and leader have allowed Brent to influence people from all walks of life throughout his twenty years in ministry.

Engaging issues such as leadership, culture, and change, Brent speaks to hundreds of thousands across the nation and abroad each year and is currently serving as vice president for Student Leadership University, a program that has trained more than 150,000 students to commit themselves to excellence.

He is also the author of *Sacred Intent: Maximize the Moments of Your Life, Reimagine: What the World Would Look Like If God Got His Way,* and *Chasing Elephants: Wrestling with the Gray Areas of Life* and is the associate editor of IMPACT, *The Student Leadership Bible.*

The desire of Brent's heart is to see people realize they have been set apart to the gospel of God, and thus, in turn, they must set their lives apart in an effort to capture every moment in worshipful service to Him.

Brent Crowe is currently serving as vice president with Student Leadership University in Orlando, Florida. He is married to Christina and has three children: Gabe, Charis, and Mercy. He holds a Doctorate in Philosophy and two masters degrees, a Masters of Divinity in Evangelism and a Masters of Arts in Ethics, from Southeastern Baptist Theological Seminary.

Notes

Introduction

1. John Bunyan, *Pilgrim's Progress* (Lafayette, IN: Sovereign Grace Publishers, 2000), 7.

2. "Pilgrim," Dictionary.com, accessed May 11, 2018, http://www.dictionary.com/browse/pilgrim?s=t.

Noon: Come Let Us Wonder Together

1. Warren Wiersbe, *Life Sentences* (Grand Rapids: Zondervan, 2007), 288.

2. John Pollack, *The Apostle: A Life of Paul* (Colorado Springs: Doubleday, 2012), 148.

3. T. Desmond Alexander, et al., *New Dictionary of Biblical Theology* (Downers Grove, IL: InterVarsity Press, 2000), 136.

One O'clock: Only the Sinner

1. Robert Fulghum, *All I Really Need to Know I Learned in Kindergarten* (New York: Ballantine, 1988), 54.

2. A. T. Robertson, *Word Pictures in the New Testament* (Nashville, TN: Broadman, 1973), Acts 9:1.

3. J. C. Ryle, *The True Christian* (Grand Rapids: Baker, 1978), 142.

4. D. E. Garland, *2 Corinthians, Vol. 29* (Nashville: B&H, 1999), 519.

5. R. C. H. Lenski, *1 & II Corinthians* (Peabody, MA: Hendrickson Publishers, 2001), 1306.

6. T. D. Lea, and H. P. Griffin, *1, 2 Timothy, Titus, Vol. 34* (Nashville: B&H, 1992), 74.

7. C. S. Lewis, *Mere Christianity* (New York: Touchstone, 1996), 114.

8. Oswald Chambers, *My Utmost for His Highest: Selections for the Year* (Grand Rapids: Oswald Chambers Publications; Marshall Pickering, 1986).

9. J. P. Louw and E. A. Nida, *Greek-English Lexicon of the New Testament: Based on Semantic Domains*, electronic ed. of the 2nd edition., Vol. 1 (New York: United Bible Societies, 1996), 568.

10. Andy Stanley, *The Grace of God* (Nashville: Thomas Nelson, 2010), xv.

11. Ibid.

12. Everett F. Harrison, ed., *Baker's Dictionary of Theology* (Grand Rapids: Baker Books, 1960), 258.

Two O'clock: From Potential to Purpose

1. M. R. Vincent, *Word Studies in the New Testament, Vol. 1* (New York: Charles Scribner's Sons, 1887), 492.

2. Rick Warren, *The Purpose Driven Life* (Grand Rapids: Zondervan, 2002), 17.

3. This statement is an adaptation of a principle taught by Dr. Ed Newton, lead pastor at San Antonio Community Bible Church, when he said, "God takes broken pieces and makes masterpieces."

4. John Pollack, *The Apostle: A Life of Paul* (Colorado Springs: Doubleday, 2012), 137.

5. For more on the name of Saul/Paul, see the article written by Dr. Greg Lanier: "No, 'Saul the Persecutor' Did Not Become 'Paul the Apostle,'" The Gospel Coalition, May 3, 2017, accessed May 11, 2018, https://www.thegospelcoalition.org/article/no-saul-the-persecutor-did-not-become-paul-the-apostle.

Three O'clock: Luke Alone Is with Me

1. The biographical sketch of Edith's life was taken primarily from the book *Under One Roof* (New York: St. Martin's Press, 2013); another article I found helpful was Linda Holden Givens, "Edith Wilson Macefield: A House Is Your Home," HistoryLink.org, July 24, 2015, accessed May 11, 2018, http://www.historylink.org/File/11092.

2. Kenneth Wuest, *Wuest's Word Studies from the Greek New Testament: For the English Reader* (Grand Rapids: William B. Eerdman's Publishing, 1997), 2 Timothy 4:10.

3. C. S. Lewis, *The Four Loves* (New York: Harcourt, 1988), 77.

Four O'clock: Head in the Clouds

1. C. S. Lewis, *Mere Christianity* (1952; New York: HarperCollins, 2001), 134.

2. John Calvin, *Galatians, Ephesians, Philippians, Colossians, I & II Thess, I & II Tim, Titus, & Philemon, Vol. XXI* (Grand Rapids: Baker Books, 2005), 206.

3. A. T. Robertson, *Word Pictures in the New Testament* (Nashville, TN: Broadman, 1933), Colossians 3:5.

4. Kenneth Wuest, *Wuest's Word Studies from the Greek New Testament: For the English Reader* (Grand Rapids: William B. Eerdman's Publishing, 1997), Colossians 3:5.

5. Ibid.

6. W. W. Wiersbe, *The Bible Exposition Commentary* (Wheaton: Victor Books, 1996), Colossians 3:5–9.

7. Ibid.

8. Ibid., 136.

Five O'clock: Getting Dressed with Grace

1. Kenneth Wuest, *Wuest's Word Studies from the Greek New Testament: For the English Reader* (Grand Rapids: William B. Eerdman's Publishing, 1997), Colossians 3:12.

2. R. C. H. Lenski, *Commentary on the New Testament: Colossians, 1–2 Thessalonians, 1–2 Timothy, Titus, & Philemon* (Peabody, MA: Hendrickson, 2001), 169.

3. Ibid., 170.

4. John Calvin, *Galatians, Ephesians, Philippians, Colossians, I & II Thess, I & II Tim, Titus, & Philemon, Vol. XXI* (Grand Rapids: Baker Books, 2005), 213.

5. Lenski, *Commentary on the New Testament: Colossians, 1–2 Thessalonians, 1–2 Timothy, Titus, & Philemon*, 170.

6. Timothy George, *Galatians, Vol. 30* (Nashville: B&H, 1994), 404.

7. Wuest, *Wuest's Word Studies*, Colossians 3:12.

8. R. R. Melick, *Philippians, Colossians, Philemon,* Vol. 32 (Nashville: B&H, 1991), 300.

9. Dietrich Bonhoeffer, *Sanctorum Communio: A Theological Study of the Sociology of the Church,* DBW 1; ed. C. J. Green and J. von Soosten; trans. R. Krauss and N. Lukens (Minneapolis: Fortress Press, 2009), 140.

10. HCSB Study Bible (Nashville: Holman Bible Publishers, 2015), 2059.

Six O'clock: From Tolerance to Togetherness

1. David Platt, *A Compassionate Call to Counter Culture* (Carol Stream, IL: Tyndale House, 2015), xiv–xv.

2. R. R. Melick, *Philippians, Colossians, Philemon,* Vol. 32 (Nashville: B&H, 1991), 89.

3. Robin Griffith-Jones, *The Gospel According to Paul* (San Francisco: HarperCollins: 2004), 449.

4. Melick, *Philippians, Colossians, Philemon,* 89.

5. Tokunboh Adeyemo, ed., *Africa Bible Commentary* (Nairobi: WordAlive, 2006), 1443.

6. HCSB Study Bible (Nashville: Holman Bible Publishers, 2015), 2044.

7. Kenneth Wuest, *Wuest's Word Studies from the Greek New Testament: For the English Reader* (Grand Rapids: William B. Eerdman's Publishing, 1997), Phillipians 1:27.

8. J. A. Motyer, *The Message of Philippians* (Downers Grove: InterVarsity Press, 1991), 96–97.

9. A. T. Robertson, *Word Pictures in the New Testament,* Philippians 1:28.

10. Paraphrased from Calvin, *Galatians, Ephesians, Philippians, Colossians, I & II Thessalonians, I & II Timothy, Titus, & Philemon,* 46.

Seven O'clock: The Spirit of Alice . . . and of Paul

1. Partially summarized from Katharine Harris, *World Bible Dictionary* (Nashville: World Publishing, 2004), 686.

2. Ed Catmull, *Creativity, Inc.* (New York: Random House, 2014), 7.

3. Ibid., 18.

4. Ibid., 29–30.

5. David Russell Schilling, "Knowledge Doubling Every 12 Months, Soon to Be Every 12 Hours," April 19, 2013, accessed May 13, 2018, http://www.industrytap.com/knowledge-doubling-every-12-months-soon-to-be-every-12-hours/3950.

6. Brent Crowe, *Reimagine* (Colorado Springs. Navpress, 2013), 173–74.

Eight O'clock: The Art of Conversation

1. David S. Dockery, *Exodus*, Holman Illustrated Bible Commentary, ed. E. Ray Clendenen and Jeremy Royal Howard (Nashville: Holman, 2015), 1277.

2. Richard R. Melick Jr., *Phillippians*, Holman Illustrated Bible Commentary, ed. E. Ray Clendenen and Jeremy Royal Howard (Nashville: Holman, 2015), 1289.

3. Andreas Köstenberger, *Colossians*, Holman Illustrated Bible Commentary, ed. E. Ray Clendenen and Jeremy Royal Howard (Nashville: Holman, 2015), 1297.

4. This section has been summarized, and at times quoted, from the notes at the beginning of each letter in the Holman Christian Standard Bible.

5. A. T. Robertson, *Paul the Interpreter of Christ* (Nashville: Broadman, 1921), 33–34.

6. Henrietta C. Mears, *What the Bible Is All About* (Ventura, CA: Regal Books, 1983), 446.

7. Robert J. Allison, *American Revolution* (New York: Oxford University Press, 2011), 32.

Nine O'clock: Grace Demands More

1. Ted Engstrom, *The Pursuit of Excellence* (Grand Rapids: Zondervan, 1982), 84–85.

2. Justin Taylor, "5 Questions with Andreas Kostenberger on Excellence," TGC Gospel Coalition, October 25, 2011, accessed May 13, 2018, https://blogs.thegospelcoalition.org/justintaylor/2011/10/25/5-questions-with-andreas-kstenberger-on-excellence.

3. Andreas J. Köstenberger, *Excellence* (Wheaton, IL: Crossway, 2011), 33.

Ten O'clock: Sanctifying Failure and Redeemed Regret

1. "Failure," Dictionary.com, accessed May 14, 2018, http://www.dictionary.com/browse/failure.
2. Wayne Grudem, *Systematic Theology* (Grand Rapids: Zondervan, 2000), 1254.
3. https://www.desiringgod.org/messages/jesus-is-precious-because-he-removes-our-guilt

Eleven O'clock: Life Imitates Story

1. The phrase "the soul's autobiography" appears in Henrietta C. Mears, *What the Bible Is All About* (Ventura: Regal Books, 1983), 201.

Midnight: Finished . . . Begin

1. John Pollack, *The Apostle: A Life of Paul* (Colorado Springs: Doubleday, 2012), 297.
2. This story was summarized and based on a story A. W. Tozer wrote about in "Born after Midnight." A. W. Tozer, *Moments after Midnight* (Harrisburg: Christian Publications, 1959), 118.
3. J. B. Lightfoot, ed., *Saint Paul's Epistle to the Philippians* (London: Macmillan, 1913), 150.
4. William Barclay, ed., *The Letters to the Philippians, Colossians, and Thessalonians*, electronic ed. (Philadelphia: Westminster John Knox, 1975), 64.
5. R. H. Stein, *Luke*, Vol. 24 (Nashville: B&H, 1992), 588.
6. W. A. Elwell and P. W. Comfort, *Tyndale Bible Dictionary* (Wheaton, IL: Tyndale House, 2001), 148.
7. Fulton J. Sheen, *Life of Christ* (New York: McGraw-Hill, 1958), 395.
8. Ibid.
9. Augustine of Hippo, *Lectures or Tractates on the Gospel according to St. John*. In P. Schaff, ed. and J. Gibb and J. Innes, trans., *St. Augustin: Homilies on the Gospel of John, Homilies on the First Epistle of John, Soliloquies*, vol. 7 (New York: Christian Literature Company, 1888), 434.
10. C. S. Lewis, *The Last Battle* (New York: Harper Collins, 1984), 228.